GHOST HUNTERS *of* AMERICA

Dan Asfar

GHOST HOUSE

Ghost House Books

The Publisher: Ghost House Books
Distributed by Lone Pine Publishing
10145 – 81 Avenue
Edmonton, AB T6E 1W9
Canada

1808 – B Street NW, Suite 140
Auburn, WA 98001
USA

Website: http://www.ghostbooks.net

National Library of Canada Cataloguing in Publication

Asfar, Dan, 1973–
   Ghost hunters of America / Dan Asfar.

   ISBN 1-894877-69-1

   1. Ghosts--United States.   2. Parapsychology I. Title.
BF1472.U6A828 2005   133.1'0973   C2005-902299-X

Editorial Director: Nancy Foulds
Project Editor & Illustrations Coordinator: Carol Woo
Editorial: Rachelle Delaney
Production Manager: Gene Longson
Cover Design: Gerry Dotto
Layout & Production: Trina Koscielnuk

Photo credits: Every effort has been made to accurately credit photographers. Any errors or omissions should be directed to the publisher for changes in future editions. The photographs and illustrations in this book are reproduced with the kind permission of the following sources: Library of Congress (p. 12, 37: HABS,ARIZ,2-TOMB,18-2; p. 48: USZ62-126602); Istock (p. 132: Nicholas Belton; p. 4-5, 176: Oleksandr Gumerov; p. 153, 187: T. Kloster; p. 97: Rene Mansi; p. 101, 104: Peter Nguyen; p. 60: A. Sokolovsky; p. 75: Greg Solon; p. 149: Ramon Villamar).

The stories, folklore and legends in this book are based on the author's collection of sources including individuals whose experiences have led them to believe they have encountered phenomena of some kind or another. They are meant to entertain, and neither the publisher nor the author claims these stories represent fact.

We acknowledge the financial support of the Government of Canada through the Book Publishing Industry Development Program (BPIDP) for our publishing activities.

PC: P5

Listen! Smell something?
—Dr. Ray Stantz, Ghostbuster

CONTENTS

Chapter Three: Unsolved Mysteries

Chapter Four: Mission Accomplished

Acknowledgments

The paranormal accounts in this volume are drawn from conversations with ghost hunters across the continent. The bulk of them were based on interviews conducted in late 2004, but also included are a few of the best paranormal investigations from my other books. I'd like to thank all involved for being so forthright about their experiences. It goes without saying that a book about ghost hunters wouldn't be possible without the people who engage in this peculiar activity. These stories are theirs. This book is for them.

Kudos to: Patty Wilson, Pennsylvania Ghost Research Foundation; Nicole Bray, West Michigan Ghost Hunters Society; Elliot Van Dusen, Paranormal Phenomena Research & Investigation; Brad Mikulka, Southeast Michigan Ghost Hunting Society; Angel Brant, Dusty Smith, Daytona Beach Paranormal Research Group; Matthew Didier, Ghost and Hauntings Research Society; David Oester, International Ghost Hunting Society; John Zaffis; Logan and Michelle Wilcox; Lucy Keas from the now defunct Michigan Ghost Hunters Society; Bill Washell, Maine's Paranormal Research Association; Michael Sinclair, Otherside Research & Investigations Of New England; Richard Smith, Paranormal Investigations of Texas; Sean Snyder; Jan Gregory, Vancouver Paranormal; Todd Roll, Wausau Paranormal Research Society and Jason Hawes and Grant Wilson of the now famous Atlantic Paranormal Society.

Also, thanks to the staff at Ghost House Books, namely Carol Woo and Nancy Foulds, who were undaunted by all the ectoplasmic mist coming off these pages.

Introduction

I remember the first ghost hunter I ever spoke with. A few years back, I was researching folklore for a book of ghost stories set in Michigan. I'd been digging up leads on the Internet when I found the web page for the West Michigan Ghost Hunters Society (WMGHS). West Michigan—that was good. Too many of the stories I'd already written were set in the far more populated southeastern part of the state; the west could use some representation. But ghost hunters?

Right. Okay. What's a ghost hunter?

I loved the movie *Ghostbusters*, especially Harold Ramis as Dr. Egon Spengler. Anyone remember the exchange he had with Bill Murray's Dr. Peter Venkman in the New York Public Library?

PETER: Egon, this reminds me of the time you tried to drill a hole through your head. Remember that?

EGON (dead serious): That would have worked if you didn't try to stop me.

Seriously. It's all about Egon.

Anyway, according to the information on their web site, the West Michigan Ghost Hunters Society wasn't a group of Michiganders stalking rogue ghosts with nuclear accelerators strapped on their backs. The organization had never gotten the chance to save humanity from Gozer, the Stay Puff Marshmallow Man or any other demonic entity. The WMGHS was a group of individuals fascinated by the paranormal, who investigated purported hauntings in their area. They went out whenever time allowed, usually at night, to see if there was any truth to the stories of the local spooks. Apparently, members of the WMGHS were able to verify dozens of ghostly sightings. Every one of them had an encounter with supernatural entities at one time or another.

At this point, I should probably make it clear that I'm essentially a skeptic. Though I've always found folklore on the subject of ghosts interesting, I've never personally witnessed anything that would lead me to believe they actually exist. At the same time, I acknowledge that for me to argue that something isn't real simply because I haven't seen it is foolish. I mean, science tells us of manifold phenomena that exist beyond the realm of our senses. There is so much that we can't see with the naked eye—cells, atoms, light particles, microwaves. Considering all the information that modern science has offered up, only a gravely uninformed individual would state that seeing and believing are consistently and unquestionably intertwined.

But still, ghost hunters? The handle not only suggests a certainty in the existence of ghosts (because if there were no such thing, why would anyone bother "hunting" them?), but that there are enough ghosts out there that people can actually "hunt" them with some measure of success. Needless to say, I wasn't sure what to expect from my conversation with Nicole Bray, founder of the WMGHS.

As it turned out, I guess there was a part of me that was a bit surprised by how perfectly reasonable Ms. Bray was. The ghost hunting was a hobby, something she pursued in her spare time, after work. Her interest in the paranormal began with a childhood run-in with what she believed to be a ghost, and though she claimed to be "sensitive" to spirits, most of her investigations were based on acquiring objective evidence of supernatural activity. Objective evidence amounts to photographs, tape recordings, temperature readings and whatever else can be presented as proof of a haunting.

That is the "science" end of ghost hunting. There is another approach, which deals with subjective indications of ghostly activity. It is in the realm of psychics, or mediums—individuals who have a kind of sixth sense that allows them to be aware of, and sometimes even communicate with, spirits. Nicole's WMGHS was a typical ghost-hunting outfit, which uses both psychic premonitions and empirical measurements to drive their investigations.

Of course I realize that I just wrote "a typical ghost-hunting outfit." The reader might ask: "what could possibly be typical about a group of people that get together for the express purpose of investigating the existence of ghosts?"

Well, the biggest news I got from Nicole was the number of ghost-hunting societies that existed in Michigan alone. There was the Michigan Organization of Paranormal Activity Research, the Southeast Michigan Ghost Hunters, Ghost Hunters of Southern Michigan, and the Michigan Ghost Hunters Society, to name a few. And that was only in the Great Lakes State.

Next time you're in front of a computer, do a web search for "ghost hunters." You might be surprised. It turns out there's a veritable subculture of paranormal research that spans national borders. From the United States to Canada to the United Kingdom to Ireland, there are countless groups of people that gather in places known or suspected to be haunted: cemeteries, old houses, roads, bridges and parks, to name a few possibilities.

Whether they're getting together in Dublin, London, New York or Grand Rapids, their methods are remarkably similar. They usually start by researching the history of the haunted site they're about to investigate. Then, when they visit the site, usually at night, they go with flashlights, tape recorders, cameras and thermometers. They may also have an EMF sensor with them, and maybe a Geiger counter. One or two of the people in the group may profess to have some psychic ability, but most of them will depend on their eyes, ears and equipment for any indication of the supernatural. After they've recorded and then analyzed, they'll usually post their findings on their web sites.

I don't mean to suggest any uniformity or general agreement among ghost hunters. In fact, the subculture of paranormal investigation is rife with acrimony and disagreement. Different societies posting different findings on the same haunted places will find fault with each other's procedures. Numerous competing theories exist as to what comprises credible evidence. Some societies swear by "orb photography" as proof of ghosts, while others denounce the floating balls of light captured on film as nothing more than camera flashes reflecting off dust particles.

Some ghost hunters are actually skeptics, setting out to rumored hauntings and hoping to disprove the ghost stories there. Other groups are composed of true believers. Perhaps just as prejudiced as their incredulous brethren, these ghost hunters conduct their investigations hoping their findings will confirm the existence of ghosts. The mission statement of many ghost-hunting societies is to simply gather and transmit supernatural information, while others claim they are able to rid spaces of any unwanted spirits. Some groups charge for investigation and removal of the ghost; others provide these services for free.

Despite the differences in their philosophies and practices, whether they know it or not, ghost hunters are actually the inheritors of a long history of paranormal study. They find their roots in the works of historic individuals who were possessed by an abiding fascination with the fate of the human spirit after death. Indeed, the practice of ghost hunting can be traced back to 18th century, when a kind and intelligent academic named Emmanuel Swedenborg went public with his ability to see dead people.

1
Historical Huntings

The Visions of Emmanuel Swedenborg

Stockholm, Sweden, December 1761

An old man sits alone in his study, elbows on his desk, head in his hands. It's nighttime, and the room is lit dim orange by the flickering flame in the hearth. Heavy shadows dance over the shelf-lined walls, which are loaded with big, leather-bound tomes in English, Dutch, Latin and Swedish. There are more books on the floor, stacked around the old man's desk, tucked into dark corners, piled up precariously against the walls. Steam billows out of a steel pot hanging over the fire, and the air is thick with the smell of roasting coffee. The man hasn't left his study for three days, and despite his housekeeper's admonishments, he has lived on nothing but bread and caffeine.

He sits with his back to the room, practically buried under a thick coat of reindeer skins, staring out through the frosted window in front of him. Outside, a winter storm is sweeping in off the Baltic Sea, and the night is alive with howling wind and whirling snow. It's the worst blizzard Stockholm has had this winter, but the old man is oblivious to it. Neither is he aware of the pot of coffee on the fire, the three candles that have just burned out on his desk, nor the wind that whistles and moans through the walls.

The man is lost in his thoughts, and his thoughts are far, far away. One look at his face confirms this. Though only the back of his gray-haired head is visible, anyone looking through the study window from the outside would see him—scraggly, unshaven and distressed, eyes turned to the ceiling, his lips twitching over a ceaseless stream of words mumbled and half-formed.

Who's he speaking to? No one. There's no one in the room. Perhaps he's praying? If so, he's praying fervently: beads of perspiration have formed on his upper lip, his brow is creased, his upward gaze is intense, unblinking. No. He's too strained for prayer. And besides, he's been sitting this way for over five hours—sitting there, still as a corpse, uttering unintelligible whispers for over five hours.

Then is he insane? The question wouldn't get too much argument from a good number of his contemporaries. Indeed, the old man's supposed dementia is a recurring subject for gossip in the Swedish royal court. For this man isn't some anonymous elder doddering in the latter days of senility; he is Emmanuel Swedenborg, who for much of his life was considered one of Sweden's brightest thinkers. That was before 1743, the year he had the dream that changed his life forever.

For Swedenborg, it was no mere dream, but a religious revelation akin to those divine visions received by any saint, apostle or revelator among Christianity's long list of prophets. In this vision, Swedenborg traveled to heaven and hell, visited with angels, conversed with God and Jesus and was let in on the divine order of the world and the universe. When he woke, Swedenborg had a mission; he abandoned his studies in science and philosophy to dedicate the rest of his life to spiritual pursuits. The world as he knew it, would never be the same again. He published book after book on spirits and the afterlife, and soon claimed he was able to take regular trips to the spirit world, where he walked the streets of heaven and communed with the spirits of the dead.

In April 1745, Swedenborg was in London finishing a book on his religious visions. It was a particularly long day of study, and the Swedish scholar found himself taking his supper later than usual. He was alone in the private room of an inn, eating and drinking heartily, when the room suddenly darkened. In the next instant, the floor was covered by a layer of writhing serpents, lizards and frogs. Before Swedenborg even had a chance to shout, the creatures on the floor vanished, replaced by a solitary man standing in a shadowy corner.

Swedenborg couldn't clearly make the man out—he was partly concealed in the dark room—but something about him felt very wrong. In fact, Swedenborg somehow knew that this was no man—this was something else, something not of this world. He felt it in the strange thrill in his blood, the sudden coldness in the room. Swedenborg could only sit in awestruck silence as the mysterious figure opened his mouth to speak. His message was as peculiar as it was succinct.

"Eat not so much," the figure said to Swedenborg, who held a half-eaten chicken leg in his hand. And then the mysterious man vanished.

Being a religious man, Swedenborg quickly reasoned that this figure was a spirit sent from God, warning him against gluttony, one of the Seven Deadly Sins.

The Swedish scientist's new passion drew ridicule and hostility from the European academic community. Nevertheless, he persisted, and over the years he took to spending even longer periods of time in isolation.

Shutting himself off for days at a time, Swedenborg lulled himself into self-induced trances, during which he would cross over to the world of the dead. The bulk of his writings were concerned with the visions and revelations he experienced during his mystic travels to the other side of the grave.

Over the years, many people witnessed Swedenborg in the midst of one of his trances. Whether this person was a friend who forgot to knock before entering his study or a housemaid who entered not knowing he was in the room, the witness would see the same thing. Swedenborg would be sitting stock-still before a table or desk, looking upward, taking rapid, shallow breaths and talking out loud, though alone in the room.

As eager as many skeptics and academics were to dismiss the scholar as a lunatic, Swedenborg's writings gradually gained currency within the community. Remarkable stories about him being possessed by an otherworldly awareness began to circulate.

One of the more famous episodes occurred during a dinner party in Göteburg, Sweden in 1759. While wining and dining with friends, Swedenborg was suddenly seized by a premonition of a great fire burning through Stockholm, which was over 200 miles away. Two days after the dinner party, a messenger arrived from the Swedish capital with news that an inferno had indeed burned through the city the night before last, exactly at the time that Swedenborg had the premonition.

The following year, Swedenborg made use of his connection to the spirit world to assist a woman named Madame de Marteville with a little financial matter. She was the widow of the Dutch ambassador in Stockholm and, having heard of Swedenborg's purported abilities, approached him about a bill for a silversmith that she was sure her husband had paid before he died. Swedenborg agreed to help, and he got the message to the deceased ambassador. Eight days later, the dead man appeared to Madame de Marteville in a dream, revealing not only the location of the receipt for the silver service, but also a diamond hairpin that she'd lost a long time ago.

In the fall of 1761, he demonstrated his abilities again when Queen Lovisa Ulrika called him to the royal court to communicate with her dead brother. Swedenborg agreed, and he returned to the queen's palace after a few days of meditation. To this day, it isn't known for certain what Swedenborg whispered into the queen's ear, but she insisted for the rest of her days that only her brother would have known what Swedenborg had told her.

Yet whatever credibility these episodes gave Swedenborg, his abilities were still greeted with skepticism. "Who is this man, to think he can communicate with the dead?" people asked. The fact that he expressed his visions in religious terms didn't do much to help his credibility. Nevertheless, for the rest of his life, he continued with his work, regularly delving into his trances, and tirelessly writing of his experiences and the religious assumptions they led to.

Emmanuel Swedenborg died on March 29, 1772. Today we might call Swedenborg a medium or a psychic— a man who communicated with the spirits of the dead. If so, he was also the first medium of the Western world who recorded, in great detail, his psychic experiences. But at the time he was considered little more than an eccentric intellectual, and aside from a small group of followers that formed in London soon after his death, he and his ideas passed with very little notice. It wasn't until 1848, over 70 years later, that the sensational experiences of two girls in the village of Hydesville, New York turned Swedenborg's writings into the blueprint of a supernatural movement that swept across Europe and the United States, turning the Swedish intellectual into a posthumous celebrity.

America's First Psychics

Hydesville, New York, March 31, 1848

Young Kate Fox decided she'd had quite enough. The knocking had begun almost the moment she'd blown out the light and gone to bed. Lying there in the darkness, she listened as it got louder and louder. "Oh, Mr. Splitfoot," the 11-year-old grumbled to herself, "please let us get some sleep."

The Fox family had moved into the small wooden cottage three months previous, and they had been forced to endure the bizarre nocturnal happenings that plagued their new home ever since. At first, it was just the noises—the sounds of someone, or something, banging and rattling against the walls in the middle of the night. Throughout the early months of 1848, John Fox did what he could to calm his wife and daughters, making nightly checks for squeaky floorboards and loose door hinges and window shutters. No matter how carefully he checked, however, the knocking would start the moment the lights were out.

John Fox was as stubborn as he was practical, and at first he refused to believe that anything unnatural was going on. But he could only hold on to this conviction for so long. His wife kept hearing footsteps in the night, creeping through the house and down into the cellar. More than once, John Fox was shaken out of bed to investigate. He obliged the first few times but stopped when he found nothing wrong in the darkened storeroom.

Whatever it was, it didn't stop at noises. Maggie Fox had invisible hands pull the blankets from her bed, and one night her sister Kate woke everyone in the house with a terrible scream when she felt two ice-cold hands press against her face. Everyone in the Fox family, even John, finally accepted that they had a ghost in the house. Over the next couple of months, they continued to endure the spirit's nocturnal activities with a stoic, if not sleep-deprived, resilience. But on the evening of March 31, the Foxes' youngest daughter Kate decided she had had enough of the nightly racket.

Jumping out of bed in exasperation, she stood in the center of the room and called into the darkness, "Here, Mr. Splitfoot, do as I do!" Then she clapped her hands together twice.

Maggie and Kate had taken to calling the ghost "Mr. Splitfoot" for some time, but this March night was the first time either of them tried speaking to it. Much to Kate's surprise, the spirit responded immediately, rapping her bedroom wall twice in return. Little did Kate, Maggie or anyone else in the Fox family know that those two taps from the darkness would mark the beginning of a supernatural fad that would sweep over the nation.

That night, the Foxes discovered they were able to communicate with the household ghost. It began when Mr. Fox asked the ghost the ages of his daughters, and it answered with 11 taps for Kate, 14 for Maggie. They developed a system in which the ghost would tap the wall once for "yes," twice for "no." Amazed at their discovery, the Foxes invited their neighbors over the very next day. As it turned out, Mr. Splitfoot seemed to love the attention, and promptly answered whatever questions the astounded villagers crowded in Kate's room asked him.

Mr. Splitfoot was also able to explain, by knocking out the appropriate letters of the alphabet, that his name was actually Charles Rosna, a pedlar who had been murdered by the house's former owners. He got his message out one letter at a time, communicating that what was left of his body was buried in the ground under the cellar. Not wasting any time, John Fox hurried down, shovel in hand. Though he found nothing immediately, he and his friends kept digging intermittently week by week. Their work went on well into the summer until they finally gave up after finding nothing but a few skull fragments. If a man named Charles Rosna was indeed buried under the house, his body was nowhere to be found.

Nevertheless, this lack of a body didn't stop the townsfolk of Hydesville from talking about the ghost at the Fox house. The home was made into a local attraction, where dozens of people came to hear the ghostly raps daily—and it didn't stop there. Word of the Fox sisters and their talking spirit spread from village to village, into the big cities, across the state and eventually throughout the country. It wasn't long before someone got the idea that a handsome buck might be made off two girls who could speak with dead people. Enter Leah Fox, the girls' enterprising elder sister. Leah had been struggling with poverty after her husband had abandoned her. Apparently, she knew a business opportunity when she saw one, and she moved back to Hydesville as soon as she heard about the events at the family home.

Under Leah's supervision, Kate and Maggie became a popular stage sensation. Within the year they were touring city to city, putting on public séances where rapt audiences watched as the Fox sisters communicated with dead spirits. It was quite a show, with moving objects, levitating tables and conversations with ghosts, many of them the spirits of famous dead. The show was a smash.

Communicating with dead people became all the rage. All over the country, the parlor room séance was suddenly the thing to do, and self-proclaimed mediums started popping up in every town and city. This widespread fascination with the dead spread over the Atlantic into Europe, and Emmanuel Swedenborg's lonely meditations upon the spirit world became popular reading.

And thus the movement called Spiritualism was born. For many people, speaking with the dead was nothing more than a diversion—séances were just a way to liven up a dinner party. Others, however, took the movement far more seriously. Among Spiritualism's more ardent followers, great faith was put in mediums, those gifted individuals who had the power to put people in touch with the spirits of the dead. In the United States and Great Britain, the popularity of Spiritualism surged whenever the numbers of dead did. In America, it reached its peak after the Civil War, when countless people eager to contact beloved family members killed in the fighting sought the services of their local medium. In the United Kingdom, Spiritualism crested in the brutal wake of the First World War.

Yet as Spiritualism grew in popularity, its detractors grew more vocal. Rational-minded debunkers everywhere sought to disprove mediums' claims. Many celebrity psychics were found to be taking advantage of the dim séance room lighting for sleight-of-hand trickery they hoped to pass off as ghostly activity. These debunkers became the first modern, bona fide paranormal investigators. They were empiricists fascinated by the supernatural, but they refused to accept supernatural phenomena until every possible rational explanation was ruled out.

The most famous of these early paranormal investigators was the Society for Psychical Research (SPR). Established in Britain in 1882, the SPR was made up of both spiritualists eager to see their beliefs stand up to thorough empirical testing and scientists intrigued by supernatural claims. The SPR subjected every séance, medium, clairvoyant, hypnotist and haunted house they came across to their rigorous scientific standards. Over the years, SPR members debunked numerous mediums and disproved all sorts of supernatural phenomena.

An American chapter of the SPR was formed in 1885. In the United States and Britain, the SPR set the standards for contemporary paranormal investigation. Whether members were skeptics or faithful spiritualists, they were encouraged to observe phenomena carefully, gather evidence meticulously and never stray from hard fact. It wasn't long before this strict scientific approach alienated some of SPR's spiritualists who favored a more intuitive-based psychic investigation. To this day, paranormal investigation can be loosely divided along these lines, where psychic investigators entering a haunted site tend to go with gut feelings and impressions, while scientific investigators conduct their examinations by collecting objective evidence—photographs, video, voice recordings, temperature readings, etc. Many ghost-hunting societies use both methods.

As proficient as the early investigators were at debunking the spiritualist mediums, no one was ever able to expose the Fox sisters as frauds. In their case, Kate and Maggie proved to be their own worst enemies. The immense success of their show didn't come without a price. Kate and Maggie's touring schedule was exhausting, and by 1855, both girls had turned to alcohol to deal with life on the road. Two years later, Leah quit as their manager, and the girls were left to fend for themselves. Soon after that, Maggie Fox became disenchanted with spiritualism and shocked the supernatural community when she quit the show and converted to Catholicism. Kate continued by herself, slogging through her now-chronic exhaustion and a growing alcohol problem.

When Maggie and Kate got together for their next tour in 1888, over three decades had passed. They went public to denounce Spiritualism as a farce and confess the deceit of their own show. They revealed that from the beginning, they had made the rapping noise by cracking their toes. Whatever they were hoping to achieve with these confessions, their statements made very little impact—true believers kept on believing.

Leah declined to comment on her sisters' claims. The response to their exposé tour was so underwhelming that Maggie quit before it was over, and Kate flip-flopped and reverted back to her old medium routine.

Three years later, Maggie took back her confession and affirmed to anyone who would listen that the psychic experiences of her younger years were indeed authentic. But by then, the Fox women were well on their way to the spirit world themselves. Maggie and Kate died within a year of each other, destitute and miserable—Kate, 56, finally drank herself to death in 1892; Maggie, 59, died bedridden in 1893.

The final chapter of the Fox sisters' story was written in 1904, 11 years after Maggie passed away. That winter, an incredible discovery was made in the old "Spook House," as the local kids called the former Fox family home. Two children playing in the cellar came upon a bone jutting out of the floor. Once again, the Fox house became the focus of the town's attention as one final dig was organized in the cellar. This time, a body was found: an entire human skeleton—*sans* a few chips from the skull—buried in the dirt. Of course, it was quickly deduced that these bones were the remains of the one and only Charles Rosna, who had haunted the Fox family so many years back. There was finally solid evidence to back the claims of the two girls whose paranormal experiences enshrined ghosts in the popular culture of America and Europe.

Harry Price:
Celebrity Ghost Hunter

London, England, May 25, 1937

Solid evidence was exactly what Harry Price was looking for when he ran the following ad in *The Times* of London:

> HAUNTED HOUSE: Responsible persons of leisure and intelligence, intrepid, and unbiased, are invited to join rota of observers in a year's night and day investigation of alleged haunted house in Home counties. Printed Instructions supplied. Scientific training or ability to operate simple instruments an advantage. House situated in lonely hamlet, so own car is essential. Write Box H. 989, The Times, E.C. 4

Many of Harry Price's peers in the Society for Psychical Research probably rolled their eyes at news of the advertisement. "There goes Harry again," we can imagine one tutting to another over tea, "up to his old grand-standing."

It was true that Harry Price wasn't the most well-liked member among his colleagues in the SPR, though he might easily be called the most famous paranormal investigator of his time, if not the entire century. Intense, charismatic and shamelessly self-promoting, Price was already somewhat of a celebrity when he joined the SPR in 1920. Having come to the venerable paranormal society with several haunted house and medium investigations on his CV, Price spent much of the 1920s spearheading the SPR's supernatural studies. His background as a stage magician and keen powers of observation made him quite skillful at detecting fraudulent psychics. Nevertheless, from the very beginning many people in the SPR weren't too thrilled about his membership in their organization.

His detractors made no secret of their animosity. They complained that he had no background in formal science, while many of them were accomplished in their respective scientific fields. They criticized his media-seeking flamboyance, which they considered crass and untoward. But mostly, they resented his remarkable success. Despite his unschooled and attention-seeking methods, there was no denying his track record. His investigations were just as scientifically rigorous as anyone else's, but his familiarity with stage magic gave him an edge in spotting the tricks of fraudulent mediums. Price was able to expose more fakes than anyone else, and the psychics who passed his investigations usually became famous for it.

As for Harry Price, the more public attention he got, the more his paranormal rivals resented him. So needless to say, many members of the SPR weren't too happy about the ad he took out in *The Times*. Yet in the coming year, those who resented Price for his fame would become far unhappier. As it turned out, his upcoming investigation of the "alleged haunted house in the Home counties" converted him into *the* ghost hunter of the 20th century.

Price had first learned of the Borley Rectory in 1929. A big brick Victorian building located close to the

Essex-Suffolk border, near England's sparsely populated east coast, the Borley Rectory was about as middle of nowhere as an English home could be. It was also crawling with ghosts.

The stories about the place began circulating almost as soon as it was built. The first occupants were Reverend Henry Bull and his family, who took up residence in 1863. Yet given the folktales that preceded the construction of the manse, the ghosts couldn't have come as that much of a surprise. According to legend, locals had warned Henry Bull against building on the site. They told him of a ghostly carriage drawn by silver horses, which was seen tearing over the area on certain nights. They also told him about the wretched nun who hovered over the grounds at night, always by herself, drifting through the darkness with a lonely, grief-stricken expression on her pale and shimmering face.

It was said that this woman was the ghostly reminder of an unholy union that occurred sometime in the 13th century. The story involved a nun from a nearby convent and a monk from a monastery that once stood on the Borley grounds. They fell in love and made plans to break their religious vows and elope. But their scheme was foiled. They were caught trying to escape in one of the monastery's carriages and were severely punished for their sins. The monk was beheaded, and the nun was bricked up in one of the monastery walls—alive.

Despite the warnings, a skeptical Henry Bull commissioned the building of the rectory anyway, not knowing that he was overseeing construction of what Harry Price would eventually call "the most haunted house in

England." The Bull family might very well have agreed with Harry Price. Soon after they moved in, weird things started happening in their home. The rectory's residents heard mysterious rapping sounds regularly in empty rooms and hallways, and disembodied footsteps made their rounds through the house in the middle of the night. Sometimes, they detected the sounds of a phantom carriage and its phantom horses galloping outside after sunset. And they saw the apparition of the pale nun more than once.

And yet the Bulls stayed on, bolstered by great religious faith, incredible obstinacy or resilience or a combination of the above. The Bull family remained at the Borley Rectory living alongside the ghosts for nearly 70 years, until Henry's son Harry died in 1927. The next pastor at the rectory, Reverend Guy Smith, wasn't nearly as accommodating and moved out after one troubled year.

Harry Price found out about the ghosts at Borley when a number of articles about the rectory were written in London's *Daily Mail*. The journalist who wrote the articles invited Price to investigate the house. Reverend Smith and his wife were still living in Borley when Price made his first visit on June 12, 1929. Price found the place to be buzzing with all sorts of inexplicable phenomena, from flying candles to falling panes of glass and a sighting of the phantom nun herself. After three nights of careful observation, séances and interviews, Price concluded that there was definitely a high level of supernatural activity in the house and swore to return.

The rectory became his pet project, and he revisited the house several times throughout the 1930s, each investigation resulting in ever more dramatic phenomena. When the house was abandoned in 1935, Price seized the opportunity to do something unprecedented in the world of paranormal investigation. In 1937, he leased the house for a year and took out his advertisement for volunteer investigators in the May 25 issue of *The Times*.

He ended up selecting 40 of the 200 applicants, and he gave each of them a book of investigative procedures he had written himself. This "Blue Book" was the first formal guidebook on paranormal investigation ever written. The book provided Borley volunteers with instructions on how to deal with various supernatural manifestations, as well as on the proper use of equipment, including thermographs, cinematograph cameras and ouija boards, which were to be used for communicating with the dead. Price outlined rigid procedures for a proper investigation and urged the investigators to keep minute records of their movements and observations. His procedures are still considered a benchmark by some of the top ghost hunters today.

As for the investigation itself, there were mixed opinions on what was actually accomplished by the round-the-clock, year-long study of the Borley Rectory. On one hand, nothing like this had been attempted before, and Harry Price was no doubt pleased about what the rectory did for his fame. He wrote two popular books on the experience, and one of them *The Most Haunted House in England: Ten Years of Investigation of Borley Rectory* (1940), was a commercial success and a landmark work in psychical research.

The book was published a year after the rectory burned to the ground thanks to the house's last resident, who accidentally knocked a stack of books into a paraffin lamp. That occurrence might not have come as much of a surprise to Helen Glenville, one of Price's 40 investigators. Glenville, who had been chosen for her purported psychic abilities, had channeled one of Borley's ghosts on March 27, 1938. Price had recorded in his notes that the spirit informed Glenville that the house would burn down that very night. Though there was no fire that night, the prophecy was realized exactly 11 months later, which added more mystery to the story of Borley—and, inevitably, helped sales for Price's book.

Price's death in 1948 revealed just how many investigators he'd upset and irritated while he was alive. Skeptical media and rival researchers piped up all at once. Highly critical of Price's investigation, they brought up all sorts of procedural flaws and inconsistencies, and they accused Price of exaggerating (read: inventing) much of the recorded phenomena at the rectory. It was true that the findings of the 1938 study weren't nearly as dramatic as Price's reports during his earlier solo investigations. And it was also true that the frequency of strange happenings in the house did have a way of stepping up dramatically whenever Price was around.

As for the romantic legend of the nun and the monk, a little bit of historical research revealed that no Borley monastery had ever existed, in the 13th century or at any other time. The closest thing was a church that had once stood on the site of the rectory in the 12th century. In the eyes of Price's critics, the fact that he'd relied on the folktale as an explanation for the apparitions of the nun and the carriage did nothing for his credibility.

Despite all this doubt, Price's highly active, if contro-versial, life's work has secured his place in the history of paranormal research. Though it has been acknowledged that many of the stories he told about his early life can't be trusted, and that he probably embellished many accounts of his investigations, there is something about Harry Price that speaks to the contemporary ghost hunter. Unlike many of the dreary academics that largely constituted the rank and file of the SPR, Price had a way of popularizing paranormal investigation.

He was a man who understood the value of a good story. He was the author of over 12 books on the para-normal, and his detailed accounts were as entertaining as they were informative. He succeeded in piquing a read-ership's curiosity in the unusual, outlandish and often eerie world of the professional ghost hunter, while weav-ing an odd sort of mystique around himself and the lifestyle he chose. Harry Price was the intrepid and ener-getic jet-setter, schooled in history and folklore, traveling around the world tirelessly in search of the unknown, melding scientific and psychic methods to uncover mys-teries most people can only marvel at. To this day, Harry Price is the idealized model of the ghost hunter. Though there were others that followed—the Hans Holzers, Tom Perrotts and Andrew Greens of the world—Harry Price was the first.

In one way or another, every ghost hunter featured in this book owes something to Harry Price. For not only was he able to attach a sort of cultural cachet to ghost hunting, but in popularizing his investigations, he also laid bare his methods, allowing others to apply his standardized approach to hauntings around the world. While many things have changed since Price's time—today's ghost hunters use every technology from infrared thermometers and Geiger counters to electromagnetic field meters and digital cameras—generally, the methods are still the same. Just like Harry Price, ghost hunters today investigate local hauntings by combining objective observation with psychic intuition. Like Price, they endeavor to rationally explore inherently irrational phenomena. And of course, just like Harry Price, they have their stories.

The Bird Cage Theatre

Tombstone, Arizona is home to a very interesting haunting that involves the notorious Bird Cage Theatre, which was established in 1881 and kept its doors open until 1889 when flooded mines and plummeting silver prices reduced Tombstone to a ghost town. During the nine years it was open, the Bird Cage Theatre was generally acknowledged as the epicenter of madness in Tombstone. In 1882, *The New York Times* described the vaudeville house as the "wildest, wickedest night spot between Basin Street and the Barbary Coast."

Every night, countless booze-soaked dramas played themselves out in the gas-lit confines of the lively theater. Soused gunslingers and lovesick miners blended their fates with ladies of the night and card players in an intoxicating atmosphere where festering resentment often boiled over into violence. The more than 140 bullet holes in the walls and ceiling of the theater, caused by the 16 gunfights that were said to take place there, attest to the raucous goings-on in this lawless community.

Closed since the last patron threw back his last glass of whiskey in 1889, the theater was abandoned for nearly half a century. It reopened to the public in 1934, and today the Bird Cage is a museum that showcases Tombstone's wilder years. Many would say that it offers much more. The first accounts of strange happenings in the theater began shortly after the reopening; it quickly became apparent that there were forces in the Bird Cage unconcerned with the passage of time.

While the first visitors to the old theater-turned-museum were treated to artifacts from a time past, many of these early Western enthusiasts were far more impressed by the bizarre and frightening phenomena occurring in the building. Early visitors were surprised to hear the sounds of a party. Distant voices singing old folksongs and boisterous peals of men's laughter could be heard faintly, and a faint whiff of cigar smoke was in the air. Witnesses would head downstairs, convinced that some sort of party was going on in the basement, but the only thing they would find when they got there was the abandoned Poker Room. The sounds of distant revelry would stop the moment anyone opened the door to this room. Chilled witnesses would later swear that there was something intangibly eerie about the silent room and its unoccupied chairs—as if, somehow, invisible gamblers were still sitting on them, waiting for everyone to leave before they commenced their game.

Other people claimed to hear the sound of a woman singing faintly in one of the second-floor cribs overlooking the main room. The singing would grow clearer when witnesses ventured up to the second floor, but it would cease before anyone could get too close to any of the cribs. Other people spoke of hearing spur-jangling footsteps walking across the main room on the first floor when there was no one there. Sometimes the disembodied footsteps would come incredibly close to visitors, passing within mere inches of them, but even then, the phantom presence would remain invisible to human eyes. Or, rather, to so *some* people's eyes. There were also people who claimed to spot the purported phantom as he made his way across the Bird Cage's main room. He appeared as a semi-transparent figure in a black suit, wearing a big black cowboy hat. Witnesses noted that he walked with a casual stride, and that his hair was black as pitch, but the apparition always vanished before anyone could discern much else.

Now, as then, many visitors claim to see and hear inexplicable phenomena. The occurrences have remained remarkably constant over the last 70 years. For the most part, what was reported then is still reported today, giving the Bird Cage Theatre as much of an allure among supernatural enthusiasts as it has with history buffs.

The theater has received a good deal of attention from paranormal societies, many of which have worked to clarify the phenomena there. According to some of these societies' investigations, the Bird Cage is every bit as haunted as witnesses have reported. While psychics have been able to detect a large confluence of restless souls, more scientifically oriented organizations have amassed many photographs, video and audio recordings suggesting that the Bird Cage might indeed house a whole group of ghosts. The Southwest Ghost Hunter's Association has reported that as many as 31 revenants might be haunting the theatre.

Angel Brant, a gifted psychic who lives in Mesa, Arizona, doesn't dispute that there are real supernatural entities in the Bird Cage. "There's a lot of ethereal energy in the building. Much of it comes from the objects on display, so many of which transmit the energy of their former owners, and then, of course, a lot of it comes from all the excitement and drama that took place there when it was open. Energy like that doesn't just go away." That said,

Ghost hunters have detected many restless souls inside the Bird Cage Theatre.

Angel herself has only ever detected one specific spirit in the Bird Cage.

"The first time I felt his presence was when a good friend and I went to visit. We were walking up to the backstage area on the main floor when we both smelled this really strong cigar odor. It was like there was someone right there smoking a big, stinky cigar, but the only people in the area were my friend and I." The pair went back down to the main floor where they saw the only other person in the theater. "We asked this man if he had been smoking a cigar and he told us that he hadn't. So then we asked him to come up backstage, just to see if he'd smell the same thing." When the trio got back to the area, the cigar smell had completely dissipated, but whoever had been smoking it apparently was still there. "Neither me nor my friend felt anything, but the guy that was there with us suddenly looked really surprised and sort of scared. We followed him back down to the main floor, where he told us that something backstage had been pushing him away by the chest. It was like there was someone there who didn't want him to be backstage."

All three were mystified by the experience, until Angel came up with an informative bit of history on the building. "It turns out that there used to be this stage manager who worked backstage," Angel explains. "During the Bird Cage's busiest time, his job was also to keep the men away from the dancing girls and the women who were in the cribs upstairs." Angel also discovered that this man was scarcely seen without a big, malodorous Mexican cigar jutting from his mouth. Angel is sure that they had encountered the spirit of this stage manager that day. It is fitting that this spirit—who guarded so many female performers from the male audience when he was alive—would hold back the only male in the trio while allowing the two women to get by. It seems that even in the afterlife, the spirit of this resolute stage manager continues to do his job, keeping the rough rabble of male visitors away from the women. "I sense that this man loved his job," Angel says. "That's why he's there—he loved working at the Bird Cage so much that he hasn't been able to let it go yet."

Murder on Skyline Drive

The haunting on Skyline Drive is one of the lesser-known ghost stories in Tombstone's heavily chronicled past. While tourists and curiosity seekers flock to famous haunted sites like Big Nose Kate's Saloon and the Bird Cage every year, the haunted house on Skyline Drive rightfully gets very little attention. The current owners of the home are not eager to sacrifice their privacy for the sake of putting another haunted location on Tombstone's supernatural register.

Thus Angel Brant is guarded when she talks about the stately old house up on the hill on Skyline Drive. "Most of us can only imagine what it would take to live in a place so actively haunted by the spirits of the dead," Angel says, "never mind putting up with the widespread attention that this sort of thing brings on." So even though Angel is more than willing to talk about her ongoing investigation of this home, all she will reveal about its location is the street that it lies on.

In the 1880s, a wealthy assayer and his wife and daughter lived in the home. This particular assayer supervised a few of the mining operations around town and paid the miners for the ore they eked out of the earth, but very little else is known about him. Angel has found no written record of his name or background. All she knows about him is what she's been able to intuit during her psychic investigations. "I keep getting an impression of the name Cliverson," Angel says. "I'm pretty sure this was the assayer's family name."

"Sometime in the 1880s, Mr. Cliverson fired a man named John Hicks, who worked in one of his mines." Angel can't say for certain why Hicks was fired, but given what followed, it's apparent that the miner wasn't at all happy about it. A few days later, an angry and inebriated John Hicks came knocking on Cliverson's door, looking for money he felt he was owed.

"Well, Cliverson wasn't home," Angel says, "but his wife and his eight-year-old daughter were." Mrs. Cliverson opened the door and found a man lost to fury. Hicks kicked the door open and sauntered inside, roaring about just desserts and money that was owed him. Terrified, Mrs. Cliverson tried telling the drunken miner that her husband wasn't there, that he was out working at one of the mines, but the man was beyond reason. In a fit of homicidal madness, Hicks assaulted Mrs. Cliverson and stabbed her to death. He then turned his knife on the eight-year-old.

The strange goings-on in the house today find their roots in this horrific sequence of events that took place over 100 years ago. "I've felt the vibrations of the little girl," Angel says. "I've felt her presence while sitting on the front porch. I could feel her fear and the pain of being stabbed." But that's only what Angel divined during her psychic investigations. Another, far more dramatic, phenomenon occurs on the front porch. Angel describes her experience sitting there with a trace of awe in her voice. "The porch, it rains slag: little fragments of rock—they come out of the overhang and shower all over the patio floor. They form on the walls and on the steps."

Angel believes the little girl is responsible for this bizarre occurrence. "I think that this is the girl's way of keeping men away. Because the time that I saw it happen, the slag rained all around me, but I didn't feel any of it— what I did feel was her being stabbed violently. I got a real impression of this poor girl's fear." According to Angel, this falling slag is the girl's defense mechanism against, men she doesn't know. More than one male visitor to the house has been welcomed with a fine mist of falling slag.

Why the front porch? In all probability, the raining rock phenomenon used to occur inside the house, before previous owners' renovations turned the living room into the porch. While we don't know what motivated these renovations, we can imagine how difficult it must have been to be constantly cleaning slag off the living room floor. Could it be that residents of the house made the living room into a porch to keep the mysterious rock from collecting inside? Or perhaps they hoped whatever force was haunting the room would depart when the room was turned into an outdoor area. They very well might have known that the girl and her mother were killed in the living room, and they could have come to the conclusion that one of the two was responsible for the phenomenon.

If so, they would quickly learn that all they solved with the renovations was their cleaning problem. The spirit of the girl continues to rain slag on the same part of the house where she met her end, continuing on, perhaps, for as long as the poor girl continues to relive the last brutal moments of her short life.

Voices in Gettysburg

Many ghost hunters recognize the International Ghost Hunting Society (IGHS) as one of the premier paranormal investigators. Headed up by David Oester and Sharon Gill, the IGHS began in the early 1990s, when David and Sharon moved into a house on the Oregon Coast. Their first experiences with the supernatural occurred in this house—experiences that have long since been overshadowed by a staggering number of ghostly encounters.

"The house was haunted by the ghost of a little girl," David Oester recalls, "and for the next two years, we experienced firsthand what it was like to live in a haunted house." David and Sharon weren't shy about what was going on in their home and spoke openly about the ghost to people in their community. "We found that the more people we talked to, about one in three either knew someone who had an experience or had one of their own," David says.

They decided to channel all this supernatural interest into a creative project and wrote a book of ghost stories. This first volume had nothing to do with paranormal investigation, but was a book of dark stories meant to creep people out before bed, or send shivers around a crowded campfire. The project held their interest, and they put out an ad in a local paper asking for people to come forward with any stories they might have.

What happened next was something of a publicity miracle. A journalist for a small paper interviewed David and Sharon about their hunt for the ghost stories, spinning a satirical article about the pair's enthusiasm for the paranormal. The story was put on the AP wire service and actually piqued the interest of producers at ABC News Nightline. People from the broadcast news program got in touch with David and Sharon, asking them if they were interested in a spot on an upcoming show.

David's response was unequivocal. "We told her 'no.' " Up until that time, the pair had limited their work to gathering people's stories and articles about ghost stories, and they felt uneasy being featured on a national television show. "We told her to call us back in six months. And, well," David says, " she did."

This time, David and Sharon agreed, and three days later the two paranormal enthusiasts had an entire television crew at their house. "We spent the day with them," David recalls, "taking them to the different sites we covered in our book, *Twilight Visitors*." The shooting went well and aired on November 24, 1994. An auspicious start to their paranormal careers, this experience would be only the first of David and Sharon's many media stints.

Nearly two years later, in July 1996, the now-full-fledged paranormal investigators posted their first six photographs of ghosts on the Internet. The response was amazing. According to David, their site saw 2000 hits in its first month, and by November of that year, they were flooded by e-mails asking how they got their photos. David and Sharon then realized that there were many people who were interested in the study of ghosts, the proof of their existence and how to become a ghost hunter.

Almost as a response to this burgeoning curiosity, the couple founded the International Ghost Hunters Society.

Operating under a mission statement that swore their dedication to the "research, documentation, education and investigation of ghostly phenomena, recorded through EVP, digital, film and video photography," David and Sharon's society is composed of "ghost believers, ghost hunters and ghost researchers."

Many were drawn to the IGHS's mission, and today David states that his society has over 14,000 members in 87 countries worldwide. As full-time paranormal investigators, he and Sharon travel the United States year-round looking for hauntings to investigate. Their annual ghost conference has been going on now for nine years. In addition, David and Sharon have, to date, written nine books on the supernatural, and they are currently working on a five-volume book series tentatively titled *America's Hauntings*.

In many ways, the success of the IGHS is a testament to the ghost hunting society's most valuable tool: the Internet. Before the World Wide Web, ghost hunting societies had no way of presenting their studies to the public, short of getting a book published. It was an obvious obstacle to ghost hunters—while some investigators were published, there was no way everyone interested in paranormal investigation could expect to publish a book. Everything changed in the mid-1990s, when the Internet became accessible to the general population. Suddenly, anyone interested in ghost hunting could go out, conduct their investigations and then share their findings with the public via their web sites. Many contemporary ghost-hunting societies got their start in the mid-to late 1990s because of the Internet. David and Sharon's IGHS led the way on the Internet, but it wasn't long before hundreds of others created their own sites.

But back to the IGHS. One of the few full-time ghost hunters out there, David has conducted so many investigations that when he's asked which ones stand out in his head, he's momentarily stumped. "Well, we do this year-round, you know," he finally explains, "so in many ways, the investigations kind of blend into one another. After a while, you notice that the phenomena follow patterns that are common to all investigations." He pauses for a few seconds before continuing. "I guess I could tell you about the voices we recorded in Gettysburg."

Gettysburg, Pennsylvania—for those shaky on their history—is the site of the worst battle the United States ever endured. Largely considered to have changed the tide of the Civil War, the three-day fight, which raged from July 1 to July 3, 1863, marked the limit of the Confederate advance into Northern territory, and put the South on a long, slow road to ultimate defeat. It didn't come cheap: by the time the Union army stood over the bloodstained battlefield, total casualties for both sides numbered over 50,000 dead, wounded and missing.

While Gettysburg has long been a favored destination for history buffs, it has also become a hot spot for paranormal investigators. David claims a good deal of responsibility for this phenomenon. He notes that his 1998 Gettysburg Ghost Conference was a seminal event for ghost hunters, and it brought scores to the region to explore the innumerable ghosts that haunt the battlefield. "When we arrived at Gettysburg," David says, "ghosts were only something they brought up in their local ghost stories. We were the ones that introduced the study of ghost photography and, over the years, we were the first ones that talked about recording EVP on the battlefield."

David and Sharon have returned to Gettysburg to host their conference and study the haunted battlefield a number of times since 1998. Now acknowledged by many paranormal enthusiasts as one of the most haunted places in America, Gettysburg never fails to provide David and Sharon with dramatic results in their investigations. Their trip to the battlefield in the spring of 2003 was no exception.

They had spent April of that year in the historic town, going out every night with cameras and digital recorders, scouring the battlefield for phenomena. Photographs and voice recordings are the two forms of ghostly evidence the IGHS is partial to, for a number of reasons.

"A lot of investigators do EMF readings," David says, referring to the procedure many ghost hunters use to measure spikes in the immediate electromagnetic field with EMF meters, "and you can do thermal scans, but what does that tell you? You've got nothing that you can document as proof after the investigation's over."

In fact, David and Sharon don't even bother taking thermometers anymore, especially when they're investigating sites outside. "It doesn't tell you anything. Not that cold spots never accompany ghosts—they often do—but when you're outdoors, cold spots registering on an infrared thermometer could easily be generated by air currents. And as for EMF spikes, they could be coming from nearby power lines."

Paranormal activity is very high in key areas of the Gettysburg battlefield.

David continues, "The most reliable method is actually working with Electronic Voice Phenomena (EVP) because that isn't something that can be created by an outside variable. Either there's a voice on your recorder or there isn't." David even prefers EVP to photography. "Say you take a picture and you get ectoplasm," he explains— ectoplasm, according to supernatural theory, being the material residue some ghosts leave behind. "Sure, it might look impressive. You've got pictures of these silver wisps on camera and it might be proof that something was going on, but ectoplasm can only tell you so much. You won't get a ghost's story from a picture of ectoplasmic mist. When you play back a recording of a ghost's voice, you can hear it speaking. You can hear its emotion."

Emotions were certainly running high in Gettysburg during the first three days of July 1863, which might explain the IGHS's extraordinary success at obtaining EVP there over the years. Indeed, when David Oester brings up how he captured ghostly voices on his recorder that April night in 2003, he speaks of it casually—as if he could be talking about any investigation on the battlefield—because he has captured EVP in the area so frequently.

"We were out around the area of Little Round Top late one afternoon, walking around the base of the hill right by the skirmish lines," David recalls. A little background, for those who aren't familiar with the details: Little Round Top, a wooded hill on the southern end of the battlefield, was the scene of crucial fighting during the second day of the battle. It was there that one regiment, the 20th Maine, saved the Union army's left flank when the men made their now-legendary stand against a Southern force of superior numbers. If the Confederates had succeeded in taking the hilltop that day, they might well have changed the course of battle—but they were not able.

David and Sharon were making their rounds over the area, digital recorders running. With the sun falling slowly over a pleasant Pennsylvania afternoon, it might seem strange to think that there'd be any spirits around to record. Neither Dave nor Sharon could hear anything unusual, and there were no misty apparitions floating around, no inexplicable cold spots or hot spots. Nor were there any audible voices to be heard.

Nevertheless, the pair continued around the hill, confident their recorders would pick up something. David disregards the widely held notion that ghosts only come around after dark. "Past experience has taught me that ghosts don't rest," he says. "If they haunt a place, they're always there, whether we see them or not." Invisible, okay—but inaudible? For those unschooled in EVP, the act of trying to record sounds one can't hear might seem absurd. Yet according to David, and many other ghost hunters, the unique frequency of EVP sound makes it inaudible to human ears as it's occurring, but quite plain when reproduced on tape or digital recorders. In so many cases, ghost hunters only hear the voices afterwards, when they're going over their recorders—knowing only then that they were walking among ghosts.

Such was the case with Dave and Sharon that spring afternoon. While they walked around Little Round Top with their recorders on, they never got so much as the slightest indication that ghosts were present—they didn't experience anything strange or unusual, and they called it quits after a quiet night's investigation. The sounds they captured on their digital recorder, however, told a different story.

From the fuzz and static of their recording, two distinct voices emerged. They were men's voices, with Southern accents inflected by urgency. According to Dave, one of them said, "The Blue Cross is trouble." The other: "They're Yankees." Dave and Sharon knew with all certainty that they had neither heard nor spoken these words during their tour of Little Round Top that day. But Dave needed to run one more test before he was sure they were dealing with genuine EVP.

According to the IGHS founder, voices in real EVP phenomenon can't be reversed; when an EVP recording is run backwards, it sounds exactly the same. Transferring the audio files from his digital recorder to his computer, Dave ran the voices through software that allowed him to play them backwards. He wasn't the least bit surprise when the two voices came back to him exactly the same backwards and forwards. It passed the EVP test—ghosts had been speaking to him through his digital recorder.

As for the question of who the voices belonged to, history provided Dave and Sharon with a large part of the explanation. Given that the men in the recording had Southern accents and referred to others as Yankees, it seemed obvious enough that the men were Southerners. The fact that the EVP was captured at the base of Little Round Top, exactly where the men of the 15th Alabama Regiment would have begun their assault, corroborated the assumption. But what did one of the voices mean by "The Blue Cross is trouble"?

Dave and Sharon were stumped. "We couldn't figure out what the heck the Blue Cross meant," Dave says today. "It was almost a month later that we were speaking to a seamstress who made Civil War uniforms, and she told us that the Blue Cross was the insignia of the 3rd Brigade, the division the 20th Maine regiment belonged to. And so the last piece fit—the disembodied voice was referring to the Union regiment held atop the hill.

"The Blue Cross is trouble." Were these the last words of a Southerner who fell under a hail of bullets? Or perhaps the words were never spoken, but formed the last tangible thought of an advancing soldier just before he was killed. Whatever the case, the words turned up on Dave's digital recorder, just another ghostly voice in the unheard supernatural din that Dave Oester and Sharon Gill are exploring.

With Age Came Ghosts

Almost every ghost-hunting group has one—*the* haunted site, *the* definitive investigation, *the* first place that comes to mind when asked about hauntings in the area. For the Wausau Paranormal Research Society (WPRS), that place is the Grand Theatre. One of Wausau, Wisconsin's most impressive historical buildings, the Grand Theatre stands as a regal landmark of arts and culture in the Midwest.

The Grand Theatre was built as a vaudeville and silent movie house in 1927; it was modified to screen motion pictures in 1932. From 1932 to 1985, the theater presented everything from Hollywood productions to Shakespearean dramas to local musicals. In 1985, the theater underwent major renovations, and today it stands as the foremost performing arts center venue for north-central Wisconsin, a shining example of what historical restoration can accomplish.

The theater is also a great example of how ghosts and history often go hand-in-hand. Almost every ghost hunter will readily acknowledge that the longer a building's been around, the more likely it is to be haunted. From the numerous spirits that are said to drift through the Tower of London, to the rows of phantom soldiers said to haunt the battlefield at Gettysburg, it is a truism that in the paranormal world, history often equals haunt.

Certainly Todd Roll, founder of the WPRS, realizes this connection. A history and political science graduate from the University of Wisconsin-Madison, Todd's passion for the supernatural fits well with his interest in history. The WPRS founder is a well-studied ghost hunter who began pursuing supernatural phenomenon in the early 1980s, with his "legend trips" to various haunted sites in Wisconsin. Todd went on to cofound "Weird Wisconsin" and complete an informal apprenticeship in the procedures of paranormal research during his tenure with the Wisconsin Paranormal Research Center. Today, in addition to being the founder of the WPRS, he's also a member of the American Ghost Society—the well-established ghost hunters' association headed by Troy Taylor, one of the discipline's luminaries.

Todd's no slouch himself. He has traveled to famous sites such as London's Highgate Cemetery and Edinburgh's Greyfriars Kirkyard to pursue his interest in both ghost lore and history. It's no accident that as one of Wausau's top paranormal experts, Todd knows something of the burg's history, and this is clear to anyone who goes on one of the WPRS's Historic Downtown Wausau ghost tours.

The Grand Theatre, one of the WPRS's first investigations, is one of the main attractions of the walking tour. No one knows when exactly the events in the Grand Theatre began, but the earliest stories date back to sometime in the 1950s. According to Todd, the first accounts involved reports from workers who complained of movie canisters moving from the upstairs projection room to the lobby below all by themselves. Soon after, stories about inexplicable electrical shorts, cold spots, disembodied footsteps and phantom apparitions began to circulate.

The stories continue to persist, which is why the members of the WPRS decided to make their first foray into the theater in July 2001. By then, there were many accounts of the ghostly events in the theater. Todd's list of the myriad phenomena that have been witnessed there over the years covers practically every kind of supernatural activity that can occur.

"Many stagehands have reported the sound of footsteps walking across the empty stage," the ghost hunter writes. Of course, those stagehands who had investigated the sounds found nothing but a vacant stage. There was the story of how a worker who was closing the theater for the night saw an apparition where the projection room used to be located, along the back wall of the balcony.

The balcony was actually a hot spot for paranormal activity. "Lights in the projection area are often turned on when no one is looking," Todd states. Once, "two staff members reported hearing voices coming from a room behind the balcony. Just like with the footsteps, a search of the area revealed no one. The two of them were the only ones in the theatre.

Other accounts involved cold spots that seemed to randomly occur throughout the building; there was one area on the basement floor where puddles would form without any visible source of water. During the latest round of construction on the building, a much-storied electrical malfunction occurred that no electrician could adequately explain. Todd recalls: "Power would mysteriously shut off in one area of the basement. Electricians would test a wire and find it live, but when they tried to power equipment off of it the same line would be dead, only to become alive again moments later."

But probably the most famous ghost sighting in the Grand Theatre involves the phantom stagehand. He is another male apparition who's been spotted more than once by people at different times. He's always seen either standing in the lighting rack above the stage or in the wings behind the curtains. The phantom has been spotted so often that the theater staff has named him Larry. Whatever his reasons for haunting the theater, Larry is apparently a fan of live drama, because he's often spotted watching players as they rehearse. He is always standing still, except for once when two individuals witnessed him descending the spiral staircase from the lighting rack and walking across the stage.

No satisfactory explanations have ever been offered for these occurrences, which have been well enshrined in the local canon of supernatural accounts. In December 2001, Todd and his group set out on one their earliest investigations, hoping to shed some light in on the phenomena said to occur in the theater.

Considering where the majority of the reported phenomena occurred, the members of the WPRS chose to concentrate their activities in two areas: on the upper floor (which included the balcony and offices) and the stage and lighting rack. The group's first visit was uneventful. Todd's report gives no indication of any localized temperature dips, EMF spikes or EVP recordings. There were certainly no sightings of an apparition on the stage. The only information the WPRS had was a photograph Todd had taken from the balcony, which showed a misty "blob" hovering around the balcony railing.

Their second investigation in early December of that year yielded far more impressive results. This investigation was all about EVP. Though nothing unusual came up on any of their cameras, thermometers or EMF meters, wherever they turned, voices seemed to be whispering to them. One group detected a murmuring noise as they went through one of the spotlight rooms. The sound didn't make it onto any of their recorders, and though it was speculated that the sound might have been coming from a water radiator against the wall, no one could say for sure.

The entity the WPRS heard on the lighting rack overlooking the theater house wasn't nearly so reserved. The voice they heard there was loud enough to have made it on tape. Playback revealed that, for reasons the investigators could only guess at, the voice said, "21." Someone's age? A significant year? A card game?

As clear as the "21" sounded on tape, Todd Roll wasn't prepared to fully rule out the possibility of human error. "It should be noted that the two team members who took the recording were speaking at the time," he states, "which could explain the voice on the tape." Todd himself isn't sure what to make of the whisper his group recorded in the northernmost spotlight room near the offices of the third floor.

Two investigators were setting up equipment in the room when they heard a hushed voice coming from the far corner of the room. It was a faint whisper, barely discernable, but they were lucky enough to have their audio recorder running while they were setting up. The playback was clear enough to qualify as genuine EVP, and it is on the WPRS web site (www.pat-wausau.org) for anyone to hear. The EVP opens with unintelligible whispering as the investigators are discussing their equipment. The two ghost hunters continue talking, obviously not having heard the first whisper. The second time the voice speaks, it's much clearer, and there's an eerie kind of menace to its hushed and hurried whisper. "Don't come back over here," it says to the two Wisconsin ghost hunters. Only a 26-second snippet of EVP, this audio recording nevertheless formed the impressive investigative centerpiece of two visits to the Grand Theatre.

The only non-auditory phenomenon observed during the WPRS's second visit was a brief sighting of a dark shadow moving across the theater's north staircase. It was only spotted briefly, vanishing before the investigator was able to record it in any way. Todd tested the angles of light and took into account the locations of the other ghost hunters when it was sighted. If this investigator hadn't imagined the brief sighting, Todd has determined that the presence of a supernatural entity provides the only explanation. Supernatural presence...could Todd mean Larry?

Todd's ghost-hunting group visited the Grand Theatre for its latest investigation on March 22, 2002. During this investigation, WPRS's most dramatic finding was provided by a night-vision camcorder set in the north spotlight room, the spot that the two ghost hunters had been told not to come back to. The camera was placed next to an EMF meter programmed to emit an alarm upon any jump in the EMF reading. "At 8:20:47 PM," Todd states, "the EMF meter detected a field, and at the same time, a ball of light moved across the bottom of the video screen."

This was the last time Todd's crew visited the Grand Theatre. Though they plan on returning, the steady number of haunts reported in their vicinity keeps the members of the Wausau Paranormal Research Society with their hands full. Meanwhile, any showings at the grand old Wausau playhouse must put up with a few ghostly spectators who will, whether the managers like it or not, continue to enjoy the performances free of charge.

2
Paranormal Alert

The Ghost That Didn't Like Ghost Hunters

Like many other ghost hunters, Dusty Smith is fascinated by history. Indeed, the founder of the Daytona Beach Paranormal Research Group (DBPRG) lists her preoccupation with the past as one of the reasons she got involved in paranormal investigation. In many ways, the ghost hunter is also the amateur historian, sifting through local folklore and digging through historical records to get to the roots of the haunted sites in their neighborhoods. Yet Dusty is quick to point out that being a history enthusiast living in Daytona Beach can be challenging.

"Daytona is kind of different in the way we treat our history," Dusty says. "In a lot of other parts of the world, people have a pride in preserving their history, whereas here, we're amazed when a building survives more than 35 years." While Daytona real estate developers make sure that not too many such buildings stand for too long, Dusty laments the way the historical landmarks of her home state are fighting a losing battle against concrete and steel development.

Yet although Daytona's historical buildings are being reduced to rubble by the inexorable advance of bulldozers, there seem to be enough ghosts from the past to keep Dusty busy. Not that she's complaining. "You know, I find the scientific end of paranormal investigation really fascinating. I mean, the questions that mount up when you're out there are just unending. Nobody's come up with any answers yet, and people have been studying this stuff forever." And yet for years now, ever since Dusty set up the DBPRG in 1997, people have been coming to her for answers to their questions about both their history and their hauntings—not such a surprise when one considers what Dusty's been up to for the last few years.

In addition to heading the DBRPG, Dusty also guides groups through her Haunts of the World's Most Famous Beach tour, taking people on a walk through some of the town's cemeteries and haunted sites. While ghosts are certainly a focus of her tour, she also uses the opportunity to educate the sightseers about the history of the town.

"The ghost tour started because of our research group," Dusty says. "Soon after we started investigating, we realized that we needed funds for all our ghost-hunting equipment." Charging per head on her ghost tour, Dusty soon had enough money and more. Still, after the DBPRG had all the necessary equipment, it felt wrong making money off the town's deceased. "I felt funny about it. It was like, here I am standing outside this cemetery, talking about these people who were gone. I just couldn't take a paycheck from it." So out of the ghost tour was born The International Association of Cemetery Preservationists, Inc.—a group dedicated to the improvement and main-tenance of Daytona's graveyards. The association has adopted three cemeteries that, despite the ravages of the occasional hurricane, are in far better shape now than they were under county care.

Founder of the DBPRG, principal guide for the Haunts of the World's Most Famous Beach tour and head of the Association of Cemetery Preservationists, Dusty might be called Daytona's resident specialist on matters paranormal.

Nevertheless, as is so often the case where supernatural phenomena are concerned, even the specialists are left clueless. That was certainly the case in the investigation of the house in Deltona, about 20 minutes west of Daytona.

Of all the haunted sites the DBPRG has investigated, one nondescript concrete block home stands out in Dusty's mind, so much so that she's just completed a book of her own about her experiences there. "A young couple contacted me by e-mail in September 2001," Dusty begins. "To tell you the truth, at first I wasn't sure what to make of it. I mean, it was full of all sorts of stuff that was kind of over-the-top. I couldn't help wondering if this guy who wrote me was for real, but I thought okay, let's check it out—do the interview and see what happens."

It was obvious from the very start of the investigation that the tenants of the Deltona home were dealing with something that the DBPRG had never seen before. Furthermore, Dusty's group and the current tenants weren't the only ones who knew there were strong forces at work in the house. During her preliminary tour of the house, Dusty discovered a garage full of unpacked furniture. The tenants told her that it wasn't theirs but belonged to the owner, who, it turned out, moved out of the place in the middle of the night in the spring of 2000, only three weeks after he purchased it. Whatever the owner experienced in the house must have left an impression, because he still gave the front door wide berth, choosing to stay in his car and honk the horn whenever he dropped by for the rent.

It didn't take long for the ghosts to manifest themselves to Dusty and her team. "Right off, we recorded hot spots and cold spots, and picked up banging sounds in the walls. This place had a real nasty haunting going on." It would only get worse.

"Basically," Dusty continues, "what started as a Friday night party conversation in eight months turned into a very dangerous situation." Yet as the phenomena in the house grew ever more dramatic, Dusty's determination to study it also increased. At first she was spending an average of two nights a week in Deltona; by the end of the case, she was there practically every night.

"It was incredible," Dusty recalls. "In that first week, we were getting activity from three of four spots at the same time. To me that denotes that there's more than one 'entity' on site. There'd be a hot spot or a cold spot in the baby's room, banging noises in the hallway and a mist forming on the back roof of the house all at the same time.

"On top of it," Dusty continues, "our EVP readings were crazy." EVP, or Electronic Voice Phenomena, is one way investigators determine the presence of ghosts. It's a common theory among ghost hunters that spirits often emit sounds that are imperceptible to human ears but can be heard when played back on audio recording devices.

"When we listened to our recorders after our investigations, there were so many voices, it sounded like a cocktail party going on." If so, no one at this ghostly soirée seemed to be having much fun. The voices sounded harried, frantic, interspersed with growling noises and something that sounded like someone vomiting violently. Every now and then, Dusty and her investigators could make out barely legible speech. Whoever or whatever was speaking wasn't too happy that the investigators were there. "What are you doing here?" they heard the voice say over and over again.

With each passing week, as the phenomena grew more and more intense, so too did the DBPRG's sense of hopelessness. Dusty recalls how lost she felt in her search for an explanation. "Three months into it, I was absolutely stumped. I did all the background history, checked all the building records and property records, and everything I could get my hands on." Nothing. This house was a standard Florida concrete block home, built in 1968, with no outstanding events in its history. She found only one death associated with the property—an elderly woman who died peacefully a few years back. Dusty and the DBPRG just couldn't see how a solitary old woman dying of natural causes could be responsible for what they were witnessing.

And then things got worse. In December, right around Christmas, Dusty was attacked. She recalls: "The tenant and I were standing next to a set of golf clubs, talking about something, when his wife came by and told him to lay the clubs down, just to keep their baby from knocking them over and hurting herself. Well, I was standing there watching him lower the bag when suddenly they just came up off the floor and slammed me right in the midsection."

The DBPRG contacted members of the ghost-hunting community for advice, including established investigators such as Troy Taylor in Illinois and Dave Juliano in New Jersey. Juliano and Taylor promptly got back to Dusty, but even these ghost-hunting luminaries were stumped, suggesting that she either consult with a psychic or get out of the house all together, before other people got hurt.

Taking their advice to heart, Dusty sent photos to Kelly Weaver, a known psychic in Pennsylvania, and then went to the tenants. With three broken ribs rattling in her chest, she decided to level with them. "I told them we could keep coming back to the house, documenting this, getting really great pictures, EVPs and video footage, but it was time for them to make a decision. They were renting. They could move out at any time. And the situation was getting dangerous."

If, at first, the family hesitated at taking these words seriously, the events of early January 2002 convinced them it was time to pack their bags. By that time, the DBPRG had isolated the most extreme activity just outside the baby's room. They set up night vision surveillance cameras inside to monitor the cradle. The footage from this camera would ultimately decide the matter for the Deltona family living in the haunted house and, for that matter, effectively end the DBPRG's investigation of the site.

To this day, Dusty shudders when she recalls the tape. "The footage opens with the mother putting her baby into the crib; she turns on the little music box on the side of the crib, gives the baby her bottle and then turns the light off. It's only a few minutes after her mother leaves. You can still hear the baby; she's barely sucking on the bottle, so you know she's almost asleep. You can still hear the music box playing—everything's fine. And then out of nowhere you hear this voice."

It came out clearly on the audio. It said: "Oh, Emmy."

But it wasn't spoken affectionately. Dusty describes the voice as neither male nor female, but something about the tone gave the DBPRG founder goosebumps when she heard it. "We stopped the tape there and played it back several times, and sure enough, it was there." Dusty recalls. "Well, the baby must have heard it too, because then the baby sat up in its crib and went 'Uh-huh?'"

What followed was a truly bizarre exchange in which the 11-month-old child spouted garbled baby talk, while something in the darkness responded with a guttural stream of growls that left Dusty's blood cold. "Then all of a sudden, on the tape, we see this gray, transparent blob of mist come from the center of the room up over the crib rail and into the crib."

That was when the child's nonchalant baby talk turned into something else. "The girl started screaming—loud. We could hear her screaming 'No! No! No!' over and over again. On the tape, this went on for 45 straight minutes. She screamed at the top of her voice for 45 minutes."

Not wasting any time, Dusty picked up the telephone and called the house. "I told them, get the baby out of her room, now, and then I headed over there as fast as I could."

By the time Dusty arrived, the parents were in their bedroom, putting their daughter's crib together. "Of course the first thing they asked me was what was on the tape," Dusty says. "I didn't want to tell them in a way that would get them upset, but I had to get across that they were in a dangerous situation and really should get the kid out of the house."

Dusty's attempts at tact were rendered meaningless when the girl came toddling into the room. "The moment

I turned around to look at her, the crib rail came off the floor, over the corner of the bed and pinned her to the floor. It took all three of us to get that crib rail off that kid."

The family didn't stick around too much longer after that. The mother took her daughter to Maryland to stay with her parents, while the father stayed behind to close up the house and find a new place to live. "He ended up staying for about three weeks, spending most of his nights at the neighbor's house," Dusty recalls.

During this period, the DBPRG heard back from Kelly Weaver about the photos Dusty had sent. Apparently the house's bad energy was able to reach as far as Pennsylvania, where Ms. Weaver was having a difficult time with the package that had been sent to her. "She told us that it took her quite a while to even touch the envelope because she'd feel physically ill whenever she would touch it," Dusty says. When she felt able to study the photographs, the Pennsylvania, psychic got back to Dusty immediately. "Basically, most of what she told us we already knew," the DBPRG founder says. "That the activity in the house was centered around the baby's room."

The forces that were in possession of the Deltona house apparently weren't happy about the baby's location. A few days after the mother and baby left, Dusty received a bone-chilling e-mail message that had been sent out from the family's e-mail address to her ghost tour's address. It contained two simple questions. Though the words were horribly misspelled and riddled with strange punctuation, Dusty could make out the questions. They asked: "Where is the baby? How is the baby?"

Dusty headed to the house posthaste, making a beeline for the family's computer when she got there. Checking the log of sent message on the e-mail server, she found no such message directed to the Haunts of the World's Most Famous Beach tour e-mail address. Furthermore, while the DBPRG e-mail had been added to the computer's address list, as the AOL e-mail server automatically does whenever an e-mail is sent out to a new address, the tour's address wasn't on this list. So Dusty believed the husband when he told her he hadn't sent out the message.

"I have to say, this case really got to me," she says. "Not only were the findings so off the charts compared to anything we'd done before, but as much time as I put into it, I couldn't find any explanation for why whatever was in the house was so interested in the baby. No clue. This case was completely unresolved."

Despite all the time and work she continued to put into the house in Deltona, she still couldn't provide any answers. "There was nothing in any of the developers' blueprints, none of the local realtor reports. I talked to everybody. I was going nuts working the case because there was no logical reason for the amount of activity that was going on in that house." By the time the husband moved out, the only explanation she was able to suggest was a half-hearted theory about the possibility of a pre-historic Indian burial ground. Dusty makes it clear that this theory was just an educated guess, based on the fact that the area was once an Indian settlement. "Who knows?" she concludes. "They didn't exactly map sacred ground on colonial maps back then."

Another family moved in after the father left. Dusty came by once to drop off her card to the new tenants; though she never heard from them, they only ended up staying there for three months. The house then sat empty for nine months, after which a single guy moved in. To Dusty's knowledge, this man still lives there.

"I used to date a gentleman who lived around there," Dusty says, "so I used to drive by the house fairly often. I did leave my card with the people next door, telling them if they have any problems they could give us a call. But we never heard anything."

The truth is, Dusty had problems letting the case go. "It became personal. We became like family, and even though I tried to remain emotionally removed from it, the things going on were so extreme that it was impossible to keep up that objectivity. What made it even harder is we weren't able to give them any answers."

Out of a need to document the events that occurred in the Deltona home, and perhaps as a way to deal with the disappointment of not being able to come up with any answers, Dusty wrote a book about the DBPRG's experiences there. If the book hasn't managed to entirely exorcise the frustration Dusty still carries over the haunting, at least she's been able to turn it into a story—and quite a story at that.

It Runs in the Family

In 1993, Logan and Michelle Wilcox were offered an opportunity they couldn't pass up: the chance to not just investigate, but live in a house believed to be haunted. At the time, the married couple had only begun to delve into paranormal investigation, and though neither had much experience in formal ghost hunting, husband and wife were already certain, beyond any doubt, that the dead walk among the living. What made them so sure? What makes any psychic sure of what he or she experiences? They just know. Logan and Michelle are both talented psychics who know in their hearts that the strange visions, vocalizations and premonitions that have visited them for so many years found their source beyond the grave.

Logan is unabashed about his psychic abilities. "I've been aware of ghosts for pretty well my entire life," he says. "It actually isn't such a big thing anymore. You know, if you're walking through the woods, after a while all the trees start to look the same."

Just three years old when he had his first psychic experience, Logan is nonchalant about the event when he speaks about it now. "My bed was in my mother's room, tucked against the wall next to hers," Logan recalls. "One night I was asleep, or nearly asleep, when I heard a yell in the night. The voice shouted: 'There's a ghost in the house!'" Simple and to the point, if lacking subtlety, the call might have been a warning to the three-year-old, preparing him for the thing that was about to change his life.

Confused, wondering if his mother had shouted in her sleep, Logan leaned out of his bed to shake his mother.

"I was trying to get her to wake up when the light appeared in the doorway," Logan says. "It was a large ball of light, I guess about four feet in diameter, just sitting there glowing in the doorway."

Incredibly Logan wasn't fearful at the sight of the orb. He just withdrew his hand from his mother's bed and stared on, enthralled. "I noticed that the light was there, but there were no shadows in the room," he remembers. "That was confusing me because I could see the light, but it was obvious that this wasn't *light* as we might normally understand it."

No sooner did the boy register this anomaly than the ball of light crossed the threshold into his mother's room. "It moved into the room, around the chest of drawers and then closer and closer to my bed," Logan says. Staring transfixed at the approaching orb, Logan felt his nerves finally giving when the ball was within three feet. "I covered up under the covers and that's where I stayed until morning, and I didn't say anything about it."

That night marked the beginning of Logan's lifelong affinity for the supernatural. Years and countless similar experiences later, Logan's grandmother told him that such psychic tendencies ran in the family. He learned that the orbs of light he was seeing were ghosts; his grandmother could see them, his mother could see them and now he too was able to see them.

And it didn't stop there. Logan's sensitivity to spirits only increased as he grew. By the time he was in his teens, his abilities were no longer limited to spotting orbs. He discovered that he was also able to hear things, such as ghosts whispering faint messages, inaudible to other people.

Eventually he also discovered that if he concentrated, he could work himself into a trance-like state where he was able to see through the eyes of any spirits present.

Ghosts were central in Logan's life. He conducted his first paranormal investigation when he was 15 years old, and when he met his future wife, he found that she too had psychic tendencies. "Michelle had only seen ghosts once or twice during her life," Logan says, "but when she met me, she said they were everywhere." A match made in heaven. Well, in Texas, anyway.

The Wilcoxes began conducting their own investigations in the Houston area during the early 1990s, and it wasn't long before these two psychics were well known among ghost hunters in the area. Eager to include individuals with psychic tendencies among their number, numerous ghost-hunting groups have courted Logan and Michelle to join their organizations. To date, the Wilcoxes have been affiliated with five different ghost-hunting groups. And yet, as prominent as they've become today, the Wilcoxes hardly enjoyed an auspicious start to their investigative careers. In 1993, they lived in a house in Pasadena, Texas, which they were certain was haunted. For a full year, they did everything they could to communicate with the ghost that lived with them. And how successful were they? Perhaps the reader can decide.

"My sister had been living right next door to this house for quite a while," Logan begins. "Everyone in the neighborhood knew there was something going in the place. The neighbors talked about things, they saw shadows creeping around the house at night, strange noises were heard from inside."

Thanks to Logan's sister, the Wilcoxes had been aware of the goings-on in the house for a good five years or so. Intrigued, they attempted to get the owners to let them investigate, but the owners would have none of it. But when that family finally moved out in 1993, Logan and Michelle sensed a glorious opportunity to live in a home they were also investigating. Many people might consider it a ghost hunter's dream come true, an ongoing investigation much like Harry Price's seminal study of the Borley Rectory. This time, however, the "site" was home. It was with much enthusiasm that they signed a one-year lease to live in the Pasadena bungalow.

Given all the stories they'd heard about the place, however, Logan and Michelle assumed that they'd experience something unusual almost immediately. But the first night passed uneventfully, as did the second and the third. As vigilant as they were, making sure they set a few hours aside each night to study their new home and focus on any energies that might have been present, nothing unusual occurred for one week, then two. And then...

"We'd been in the house for about three weeks," Logan recalls. "We'd just put the kids to bed, and Michelle and I were on the couch, flipping through channels on the TV, when we heard sounds like thumping coming from the hallway. Like someone was stomping up and down the hall-way—really slowly."

It was what they were waiting for. They switched off the television and immediately went out to the hallway. "As soon as we got there, the noises stopped," Logan says. "We went to the kids' rooms to make sure they were still in bed and everything was okay. They were asleep."

A young female spirit wandered the Wilcoxes' home at night.

Lingering in the hallway for a while longer, Logan and Michelle tried opening themselves up to any spirits in the house. They asked questions out loud, hoping for some kind of response. Nothing.

"We eventually went back to watching TV," Logan continues, "and then it started again—the footsteps. Now the doors were opening and closing as well. The kids' bedrooms, the bathrooms, the doors were creaking open and closed." Husband and wife bolted up again, expecting this time to see some sign of the supernatural culprit, but again there was nothing. "We could hear it, whoever it was, from a distance, but it wasn't talking to us. Whenever we went out looking for it, it stopped, vanished." Without a trace—there was no evidence, physically, or even psychically, that anything was there.

"This started going on night after night, and kept going on and on," Logan says. If they still had no idea who the ghost was, at least they knew one thing: it wanted attention. Every night, as Logan and Michelle were settling down for sleep, it would start. "The kids' bedroom doors, the bathroom doors were all opening and closing. Every night we'd go to check it out. The kids were always dead asleep, so we knew it wasn't them. And we still couldn't track down what this was. It wasn't presenting itself."

This spirit's activities were reminiscent of a small child. It began with footsteps in the hallways, away from the parents, disappearing without a trace whenever either of them investigated. But the shy child became emboldened. "One night we were in our room trying to get some sleep, and this thing started up again, as usual, on the other side of the house, walking up and down the hallways, opening and closing doors." On this night, however, the thing in the Wilcox house did something different. "For the first time, we heard it walk out of the hallway, into the kitchen and up to *our* bedroom door," Logan says. "It opened *our* bedroom door, and this time, we sat there thinking we'll let it come in, we don't want to scare it—but we ended up sitting there for an hour, and nothing else happened that night."

As time went on, the disembodied footfalls took tentative steps into Logan and Michelle's bedroom, but the moment they turned on the light, the footfalls would stop, and the couple would be staring at nothing but an empty room. "After a month of this," Logan continues, "it got comfortable enough that it started crawling into bed with us. You could see the covers move, you could see the indentations in the bed. It would crawl up in there with us, next to my wife, and just lay there." The size of the indentation in the bed and the way it felt to Michelle, who'd taken to stroking its hair as it lay next to her, gave them their first hint at what the ghost might be. Michelle told Logan that it was a child after all—a shy girl that seemed to have grown attached to her.

Shy at first, that is. After a few months of sleeping next to Michelle, the phantom child seemed ready to assert herself. Logan remembers her first appearance: "We were having a barbecue over at our place, and there were about six or eight couples over. Everyone's kids were out playing in the park across the street, and we were all sitting in the living room talking." Logan goes on to stress that the kitchen, visible from the living room, was empty. He, Michelle and all of their guests were either in the park or in the living room. So there was no mistaking what happened next for anything but what it was—weird.

"All of a sudden, a row of the dishes came flying off the kitchen counter. They came flying off so hard that some of them flew into the living room area." The Wilcox's guests, instantly spooked, ran out to the front of the house. "Well, we were all standing out there. Our friends were asking all sorts of questions, and they were really bothered by what'd just happened. After a while, Michelle and a friend of ours decided to go back in to take a look."

"Now this friend of ours did not believe in ghosts, but when he and my wife walked into the kitchen, they both saw her. She was this blonde-haired little girl in a dress standing there laughing. They could tell right away too that she wasn't a normal child 'cause they could see right through her." The girl remained for several moments before vanishing suddenly right in front of Michelle and their terrified friend.

"All of our guests left pretty quick, and that was the last time we saw any of them in that house. They were too afraid to come over; what happened really freaked them out." From that day on, the little girl with the blonde hair got bolder and bolder. "Michelle's sister came over to stay with us for two weeks, and during that whole time, she told us about the girl she saw in the hallway, and at night, when she was trying to sleep, how she often felt someone's breath on her."

Logan's sister-in-law seemed to be able to put up with this situation, but things quickly changed when the Wilcoxes left her alone in the house. "We had a little family trip planned—we were going to go away camping for three days," Logan says. "But we got a phone call the night we left, telling us to come home; she needed us there. So we went back and she moved out that weekend." To this day, Logan doesn't know what happened to his sister-in-law. "She never discussed it with me. I know she spoke with Michelle about it, but I understood that it was something that was kept between the two sisters."

The phenomena in the house continued to get more dramatic. "This girl started throwing stuff around regularly," Logan says. "It got to the point where we had to use plastic dishware because she was breaking everything else. The footsteps continued around the house night after night, and she still climbed into bed next to my wife." And every night, whenever she appeared, Logan and Michelle attempted communicating with the spirit. They asked her questions. Who was she? Was she scared? Why was she there?

Despite Logan's considerable psychic abilities, the girl never answered him, and when she spoke with Michelle, it was never revealing. "She always spoke on a really basic level," Logan says. "It was impossible to get anything out of her. All we knew for sure is that she liked our daughter and Michelle reminded her of her mother. That was it."

They couldn't find anything out about this girl, even as her manifestations continued to get worse. "I started hearing screams every now and then. It was a girl's scream, and it always came from the other side of the house," Logan says. "The scream didn't sound afraid, but angry. It sounded like she was incredibly frustrated." Yet despite all their talents, neither Logan nor Michelle was ever able to find out what the girl was frustrated about. For two people so confident in their dealings with spirits, their inability to communicate with this one was a humbling experience.

At the center of Logan's understanding of the supernatural is a belief that ghosts are spirits of people who are trapped after death—spirits that, for whatever reason, haven't been able to cross over and are stuck here.

According to the belief, some of the ghosts are stuck here without even knowing it. One of Logan's goals when communicating with spirits is to help liberate them from whatever is keeping them chained to the world after they've passed. He does what he can to help them cross over.

Yet it was impossible to help the little girl who haunted their Pasadena home, because neither of the Wilcoxes were able to get through to her. "We couldn't pin down the girl's story," Logan says with frustration still evident in his voice years after the fact. "Even our research into the place turned up nothing we could hold on to."

The house itself, built about 50 years ago, didn't have any history to speak of. And while the neighborhood had a violent background, with a homicide in the early 1980s and another in the 19th century, there were no young, blond girls involved in either of these crimes. Simply put, the two psychics didn't have a clue.

"We ended up moving out of the house," Logan says. "Basically, when the lease came up, Michelle especially had had enough. Her way of thinking was, 'Okay, we've put up with this for a year, and we haven't gotten anywhere on it. It's time to let it go.'" Logan had to agree. "All we had was confirmation that the ghost was a girl, we had a whole lot of witnesses to back us up, and we knew that she missed her mother. Other than that— nothing. We didn't know why she was stomping around at all hours, what it was with her opening and closing doors, why she was throwing plates around and what the screams were about."

So it was that the Wilcoxes moved out of the house when their lease expired, leaving the young girl alone with whatever it was that was keeping her there. The Pasadena house remains one of the rare cases where Logan and Michelle were stumped by the supernatural. For all they know, the ghost of the little girl still haunts the Texas bungalow, and considering how unwilling she was to communicate with them, maybe that's the way she likes it.

House Possessed in Livonia

From time to time, Lucy Keas has been called on by people of metro Detroit to look at homes they suspect might be haunted. Though Lucy does not affect an ability to rid any abode of undesirable spirits, she has been able to give distressed homeowners information regarding what to do when they are faced with situations beyond their experience. Yet these investigations have not been all about the supernatural; indeed, Lucy has learned as much about human nature as she has about the paranormal while investigating other people's homes. When actual ghosts have been lacking, hoaxes, cons and neurotics have abounded, and Lucy has spent more than her fair share of time investigating the motives of beings that still reside on this side of the grave. She was in for quite a surprise, however, when she answered a call from a family living in Livonia, a suburb on the western outskirts of Detroit.

"It was an experience that no one would believe unless they were there," Lucy says, a trace of awe in her voice as she recollects her experiences in the house.

True to her policy of maintaining homeowners' anonymity when she conducts private investigations, Lucy discloses neither the building's street address nor the residents' names when she speaks of the home in Livonia. Given what transpired in the house during Lucy's three visits, the owners of that place are probably quite grateful for her integrity. "What we thought was an extremely active poltergeist," Lucy recalls, "turned out to be something much, much, worse."

The Michigan Ghost Hunting Society (TMGHS) visited the home three times during their week-long investigation in March 2001, at which time they observed what Lucy calls "the crème de la crème" of her supernatural experiences. "I was contacted by the owner," Lucy says, "because she really didn't know what to do anymore; she was on her last straw." Lucy and her team found out exactly why after spending their first night at the house. "We were there from nine o'clock at night to five o'clock in the morning on our first night. What I saw there on that night made every other poltergeist activity I'd ever witnessed before look like nothing."

The ruin visited on the house suggested the presence of a very strong and very angry poltergeist. "It was absolutely unbelievable," Lucy recalls. "Throughout the entire night, I made sure that we kept up a controlled environment. The two parents and son who lived in the house were always in plain sight. I wanted to keep the variables down to a minimum so there would be no question as to who was touching what."

Her efforts at controlling the environment ensured that the noises coming from the other rooms in the house were not a result of any human intervention or hijinks. But then again, whenever the group would run into whatever room the racket was coming from, the sight that greeted them could not have been produced by human hands. "When I say that these rooms were trashed," Lucy says today, "I'm putting it mildly."

According to the ghost hunter, every single item in each room would be "taken down, moved, flipped over, hid in the refrigerator or jammed under the carpet" at some time during the night. "Things would be rearranged in ways that were physically impossible to balance." Lucy recalls glasses "perched on top of forks which were standing on end." The television, originally in the living room, would somehow relocate to the top of someone's bed. Kitchenware would disappear from where it belonged and then rematerialize somewhere else. Light bulbs screwed into sockets were heaped into the toilet, and unplugged household appliances would suddenly come to life." One room at a time, the house was reduced to shambles.

If this wasn't unnerving enough, the group in the house heard whistling coming from the other rooms, beckoning Lucy and her entourage to witness the new destruction. "They made this noise, it sounded like they were calling dogs with a whistle. Every time, they knew we would come running to see what they had done."

Lucy now refers to the supernatural perpetrators of the destruction as "they," but she did not always assume that she was dealing with more than one spirit. Initially, Lucy believed that a small family that had previously lived in the home had experienced some kind of tragedy, and that the presence of the new family—mother, father and son—spurred the memory of some extreme emotional trauma suffered by the first family. This tidy enough theory did not hold. While Lucy could not find evidence of any dramatic history, events in the house suggested that they were dealing with something far more sinister than she had originally surmised.

"The difference between poltergeists and regular spirits boils down to a higher level of consciousness. Poltergeists are conscious, interactive spirits," Lucy explains, "they're usually attracted to people rather than places, and they'll play you like a game of chess." Lucy pauses briefly, making sure she chooses her next words carefully. "Demons, on the other hand, represent a much graver mental and physical threat than poltergeists. Their one purpose is to drive you out of your mind so that they can take over."

More than one occurance hinted that the small family in Livonia was dealing with forces of a more Biblical bent. For example, there was the spirits' predilection for one passage in the gospel. "There was one room with a Bible in it, and whenever that room was trashed, the Bible would be open to the same page. It was in the Book of Isaiah, Chapter 47, Verse 3." The passage reads: "Revealed is thy nakedness, yea, seen is thy reproach, Vengeance I take, and I meet not a man."

As the night progressed, Lucy managed to get some additional information from the family members. She discovered that they had similar experiences in their previous home, though the events there were not as dramatic as in their current house. The parents told Lucy that they believed "something their son had done" brought on the vengeful spirits. To protect her clients, Lucy has withheld what exactly that "something" was. Furthermore, the family told Lucy that they had called a priest before they spoke to her, and that a man of the cloth came in to bless the place a few days' before. The activity had actually gotten worse since the priest had visited.

By 5:00 AM, Lucy had determined that it wasn't ghosts, but demons, which were wreaking havoc in the Livonia home. "It was time for us to go, so I requested a reprieve for the family, asking the forces there to leave the house alone for at least 24 hours." The family was granted the time, but when the disturbances began again, they were worse than ever.

Lucy visited the house for the second time a few days later. She was shocked at the sight that greeted her when she got there. It seemed like the parents at the home had invited everybody they knew to witness the investigation that night. "It was a complete circus," the ghost hunter recalls, "none of their friends and family believed what was happening, and they all wanted to be there to see it for themselves." Of course that would be the night when the family's tormentors decided to lay low. "We really didn't get anything done. We couldn't—there were just too many people there." All Lucy detected that night were traces of "different smells," but nothing happened that came close to the bedlam during their first night at the place. The investigation turned into more of a social call than anything else, and Lucy found herself conversing with a room full of people who were content with meeting a ghost hunter even if they couldn't witness any real-life ghosts.

But things quickly got worse for the family after all their guests left. By the time Lucy dropped in for her third visit two nights later, the family was desperate. "That was the night I told them they should call in another priest," Lucy says. But even as the clergyman was walking through the house reciting prayers, the unholy activities continued. It was then that Lucy decided that a formal exorcism was the only solution to the problem.

The next day, a priest from another church paid the family a visit to perform the lengthy ritual of exorcism.

Lucy spoke to the woman of the house two weeks after the exorcism was done. "She claimed that the house was very quiet," Lucy says. After that, TMGHS never heard from the family again—with exception of the son, that is.

"The son actually tried to call me once, about three weeks after," Lucy remembers. "I knew something was wrong, but when I called him back, I never got a response. So I asked the daughter of a friend of mine, a girl who went to school with the boy, to talk to him for me, to tell him that I was here for him if he wanted to talk. Apparently, he didn't react well when my friend's daughter approached him. He told her that he didn't know what she was talking about, and that he didn't want to speak to her again. So whatever actually ended up happening in that house, I'll never know."

Members of TMGHS have had plenty of time to mull over what went on with that family. Lucy's group came up with a theory that countered the parents' assertion that it was something their son had done. Yet that theory will remain locked in TMGHS' vaults, protected for purposes of client confidentiality. "We know what the incidents stemmed from," Lucy says, "and it did not happen because of the son. One of the other adults was responsible— that's all I'm willing to say."

A Call for Help

Patty Wilson's first reaction was surprise. "I'd met Marianne a year before when she was writing an article on our organization for a local paper," the cofounder of the Pennsylvania Ghost Research Foundation (PGRF) says. "While she was interested in what our group did, she'd made it clear that the study of ghosts wasn't for her. She said she didn't feel comfortable messing around with that sort of stuff." That had been in the fall of 2002, and Patty hadn't spoken to Marianne for a whole year when the student journalist e-mailed her in late September 2003. The subject heading of Marianne's e-mail read: "I need help."

Marianne had just started the school year at Penn State University, but given her circumstances, studying was the last thing on her mind. The problem was her new residence—it was a nightmare come to life. Three weeks in her new home had driven her to wit's end, and as uncomfortable as she was about "messing around" with the paranormal, she'd become convinced that there was no other choice. Marianne felt that Patty and the PGRF were her only alternative.

While Patty Wilson's insatiable curiosity for all things supernatural impelled her to answer quickly, her concern for the distraught young woman pressed her to act even faster. That night, they spoke on the telephone, and Patty put together an investigation team for the coming weekend. "This was a totally cold site for us," Patty says. "Usually when I approach a haunting, I make sure to get all the research and eyewitness interviews done before I bring my investigators in. But this time, because Marianne was in such bad shape, we rushed in without knowing anything about the place."

Luckily, the spirits in this State College duplex were anything but shy, and Patty's group collected impressive data from its first foray into the house. "There were five of us that made it out that Saturday," Patty begins. "Scott, John, Linda, Don and I." The ghost hunters met Marianne at the door along with her friend Scott G., her roommate Adrian and her roommate's boyfriend Jason; all of them had experiences with the spirits in the duplex.

After the PGRF cofounder Scott Crownover set up a video camera for Patty to conduct her interviews, he went up to the second and third floors with the rest of the team to begin the investigation. Meanwhile, Patty started interviewing the four people. "Basically, the story was that there was a black shadow entity on the second and third floor of the house that was extremely aggressive," Patty says. "It began with the noises—with footsteps in the hallway and knocking sounds on the floor and walls."

At first, Marianne and Adrian did their best to play down these noises. They told each other that they were probably just coming from the other duplex suite, where five students were currently living. Marianne, especially, was eager to believe this explanation—until the weekend she spent in the house alone. The entire building was empty, with neither Adrian nor the five boarders in the other suite. All that night the footsteps came and went, making their way from the hallway above, down to the second floor to her doorway and back up again. Marianne did not feel comfortable in the house again. And from then on, things got progressively worse.

But as bad as it was for Marianne, her experiences were nothing compared to what Adrian went through. "Adrian was actually psychic," Patty says. "She's been able to see ghosts since she was four years old, and she knew the place was haunted when she and Marianne moved in." Why then would she choose to live in a place that was haunted?

Patty explains, "Adrian told me that if she spent her time avoiding ghosts, she'd never do anything or go anywhere. She saw ghosts everywhere." Nevertheless, the young woman had never grown comfortable with her ability. All her life, her father, a religious Presbyterian, had actively discouraged her from talking about her visions; he'd told her that the things she was seeing were the result of brain damage from a neonatal illness. A lifetime of doing her best to suppress her inherent ability had made Adrian into a meek, unsure girl. "Just by her body language, it was obvious she was scared," Patty says. She sensed right away that Adrian was uncomfortable talking about what was going on in the house.

"She told me that ghosts had always looked like shadowy people to her," Patty says. "Sometimes they were lighter, gray-colored, with clearly defined features, while other ghosts were much darker, appearing as black, fuzzy shapes. Adrian had learned to avoid the black shapes. They were the ones full of negative emotion, the ones that were bad."

Patty learned that the black shadow upstairs wasn't the only spirit in the house. When Adrian had first come to the duplex, she saw a darkened face staring at her from the basement window. Once inside, she sensed another entity on the first floor; unlike the dark shape upstairs, this one was a light shadow, which seemed harmless, almost shy. Adrian didn't feel threatened by it in the least. But upstairs was a different story all together.

Adrian was far more scared than her roommate; the thing on the second and third floor had taken an obvious liking to her. It was focusing its attention on her, almost like an obsessive stalker. "It appeared numerous times to Adrian, literally challenging her," Patty says. "One night, she'd just come out of the bathroom when she saw it step out into the hallway. It was standing between her and her room, almost like it was daring her to walk through it."

Though the shadow was dark and its features were obscured, it was obvious by its silhouette that the apparition was the spirit of an obese man. Adrian spoke haltingly as she told Patty about her other run-ins with the spirit. "Once, when she was alone in her bedroom, she was seized by the feeling that there was something in her room. In the next instant, she felt something touching her—it was running its hand up her leg."

As angry as she was frightened, Adrian spoke sternly, demanding it leave her room at once, invoking Jesus, God and the Holy Spirit. The spirit left her alone then, but it came back. On its next visit, it hovered by her bedside, pleading for her to touch it. It was on this night that Adrian realized how sad this spirit was. As repulsed as she was by its advances, she also found herself overcome by pity. Momentarily torn between fear, revulsion and sympathy, Adrian found it that much harder to order the ghost out of her room on this second time.

Marianne, however, wasn't nearly as sympathetic. Faced with having to share her living space with an uninvited inhabitant, she was angry about being afraid in her own house. That was certainly easy for Patty to understand, and she made a suggestion that many other ghost hunters would shy away from—exorcism. Patty knew someone who might be able to expel this ghost, but she made it clear that if Adrian felt at all remorseful or uncertain about expelling the spirit, the cleansing wouldn't work. "I could relate to Adrian," says Patty, who also tends to be sympathetic to lost souls. "But I told her that no matter how messed up this spirit was, it had no right to violate their personal space or scare them the way it was."

Their conversation was interrupted by the arrival of the rest of the PGRF team from upstairs. The team's preliminary sweeps of the second and third floors turned up several photographs with balls of light. One "cubby hole" on the third floor showed strong potential for paranormal phenomena, and the group set up an infrared video camera to cover the space. They also swept the area with voice recorders, asking questions aloud in the empty rooms, scouring every corner for EVP.

"John is our best EVP man," Patty says. "I don't know what it is, but he's got this knack for getting voices on his recordings. You could be standing right next to him with your own tape running and come up with nothing, while John comes up with all sorts of results." Such was to be the case again today.

While everyone else was talking, John had his headphones plugged in, listening carefully to the audio recordings he'd taken upstairs. Patty noticed him start in excitement. "John pulled off his headphones and shushed us all," Patty recalls. "He'd gotten something." John played back the recording for everyone to hear, and sure enough, it was there. Right after Scott and John were heard asking the spirit to give them some sign if it was there, the sound of someone whistling came through clearly. Modest though this piece of EVP was, it was promptly followed by a far more startling audio recording. This time, after John was heard asking a question, a hoarse male whisper sounded over the speakers. There was a harsh breathing sound, followed by the name "Glen." A few of them thought they could make out the words "I am" in the breathy recording, but they couldn't be certain.

Was this an introduction? Was the ghost named Glen? Whatever it was, the voice had quite an impact on Marianne's roommate. "Adrian fell apart as soon as she heard the voice on John's recorder," Patty recalls. "She just slid to the floor with her face in her hands and began to cry. She just said 'I'm not crazy,' over and over again."

Patty decided it was time to meet Glen herself, and she went up to the third floor. "I went upstairs with Linda," Patty says. "We were sitting on the floor with our audio recorders on. There was no furniture, nothing; the rooms were completely empty. Linda was sitting where John had picked up the EVP. All of a sudden, she says, 'There's somebody here with us.'"

Before Patty had a chance to ask her how she knew this, Linda began to sob. Spontaneous tears weren't typical of this PGRF ghost hunter. "Now, Linda's been with our organization for almost three years," Patty is hasty to add, "and I've never seen her do anything like this. There were times in the past when she'd say she had a weird feeling about a place, but she'd never channeled a spirit before, and none of us had any reason to believe she was psychic in any way."

"I'm so sad right now," Linda whispered, still crying. "I'm so sad and I don't know why!"

Patty noted that there were tears flowing down Linda's cheeks, but her eyes looked completely unemotional, as if she was completely detached from the emotion she was feeling. Her next words made even less sense than her tears. "I'm so big," the petite woman sobbed to Patty, "and everyone's making fun!" There was a pause, and then Linda spoke again. "I'm sorry, Patty," she said. "I'm saying all this stuff and I don't know why."

Patty was concerned with what was happening to her investigator. "C'mon," she said to Linda, "we're going downstairs. Whatever's up here is affecting you really bad.'" Guiding Linda out of the room, Patty was right there when the tears stopped. "As soon as we stepped out into the hallway, she was back in control," Patty says. "She looked at me straight and told me she was fine. 'I don't know what was in that room,' Linda said then, 'but as long as I don't go back in there, I'm fine.'"

Patty was deeply disturbed by what the girls living there were going through, particularly Adrian. Before she left that day, she told the pair that she'd look into bringing a woman she knew who would be able to do something about the ghost. But Adrian, incredibly, wasn't sure she felt right casting the spirit out of the house.

Patty knew she was delving into territory that many ghost hunters shy away from. First and foremost, paranormal investigators are observers, keen on studying supernatural phenomena but far less eager to meddle with it. If she was going to go ahead with what she had planned, she knew she would cross a line, and that many of her colleagues wouldn't follow her there. In fact, PGRF cofounder Scott Crownover was one such investigator, and he made it clear to her that he'd have nothing to do with any kind of exorcism.

But Patty felt strongly enough about the haunting that she went ahead with her plans to contact Nancy, the woman she knew who would be able to deal with the situation (not the same Nancy who belonged to the PGRF). Nancy agreed to go to the haunted home but told Patty that her efforts would be useless if Adrian was unsure about it. Also, if Nancy limited her cleansing to Marianne and Adrian's half of the duplex, the ghost would simply move over to the other suite, so the residents there would still need to deal with the problem. Patty was resolved to visit the students living in the other suite during her next visit.

That Monday, Patty got a call from Marianne with some incredible news. Inspired by PGRF's findings and the desire to get to the bottom of the haunting as quick as they could, Marianne and her friend Scott had gone to the State College courthouse to find out more about the house. When Marianne called Patty, she was still buzzing with excitement. It turned out that the information she and Scott had uncovered corroborated everything they found out on Saturday.

According to the records, the house was previously owned by two sisters, Eleanor and Margaret Glenn. Further research revealed that both the Glenn sisters were unmarried; they were charitable ladies who spent much of their time as caregivers in the community. Both sisters lived in the house from 1932 until their deaths—Eleanor died in the home in 1942, Margaret in 1978.

Marianne was practically breathless when she told Patty the next bit of information that she and Scott had found. For a short time, the Glenn sisters had taken care of a relative named Thomas. A young man with a severe weight problem, Thomas moved in with the Glenn sisters when his weight made him unable to take care of himself. He died shortly after he moved in.

Marianne couldn't believe it: the Glenn sisters, the voice they captured on EVP, the corpulent black shadow stalking Adrian, the obese young man named Thomas. There were too many parallels for coincidence. More than ever, she wanted the ghost out.

The PGRF's next visit was an overnight session, and though their findings this time were minimal, Patty learned some interesting things when she visited the students living in the suite next door. When Patty introduced herself and explained what she would do the next morning, she was eagerly greeted by four of the girls living there. "They'd just had a pretty scary night on their side of the building," Patty says, "and were happy that it wasn't just them." Neither Marianne nor Adrian had spoken with the residents there, and they had no idea the same things were going on.

Young college girls will always have admirers—even from spirit world.

The ghost manifested itself in the neighboring suite the same way it did with Marianne and Adrian. It left footsteps on the second and third floor hallways, knocked on the walls and jostled bedroom doorknobs. And as with Marianne and Adrian, one of the residents had the unlucky privilege of being the focus of the spirit's attention.

"Her name was Anna," Patty says, "and she was an exchange student from Sweden. Anna actually looked a bit like Adrian; she was an attractive girl with blonde hair and a slim build." The creepy and corpulent apparition obviously had something for blonds; Anna was having experiences that were as bad as, if not worse than, what Adrian was enduring. "This thing would turn off the water when she was in the shower; it would pull at the shower curtains. More than once, she caught sight of it in her bedroom when she was changing."

It was decided that they would go ahead with the cleansing. Patty called Nancy that day, and plans were made for Saturday, less than a week away. When Patty made the drive to State College, however, she discovered the plans had changed. Marianne wasn't there and neither was Nancy, but Marianne's mother was. "It was clear that her mother was really worried, and she had instantly insisted that her daughter move out," Patty says. "Marianne left that week without us knowing."

As for Nancy, the psychic would later tell Patty that she tried making it to the house that morning, but her car—a brand new automobile with no prior mechanical problems—wouldn't start. "It was the strangest thing," Patty says. "Her car just wouldn't start, though it worked fine when she tried again two days later."

Strange indeed—strange enough to prompt questions about the possibility of ghosts with mechanical inclinations. Could it be that Adrian's spiritual stalker had fixed it so Nancy wouldn't be able to make it to State College that Saturday?

Whatever the case, Adrian decided that day that she didn't need to have the spirit cast out of the house. "With Adrian, I think the thing she needed most was validation," Patty says. "She needed definitive confirmation that the things she was seeing were real." In this sense, the PGRF's work was a great help. They confirmed that there really was something to Adrian's visions, and their investigation helped to uncover the ghost's origin. The moment the looming black shadow became Thomas Glenn, it lost much of its menace for her, and became more an object of pity than anything else.

"Adrian ended up moving out of the house not long afterwards, and since we never heard anything from the girls on the other side of the duplex, we've reason to believe the spirit had stopped harassing them," Patty says. Had the ghost of Thomas Glenn finally decided to stop harassing attractive young women? Patty has her theories.

"It very well could have been that Adrian was the drawing card," the PGRF cofounder says. "Because she could see it, and it could communicate through her, it might have gotten empowered when she was there." Though she tried to do some follow-up research to determine whether or not it had a history of the kind of things that had gone on when Adrian was living there, Patty quickly encountered a number of challenges.

"It was very difficult because students move from year to year—often they're not in the same apartment for the same year even," Patty says. "So it was hard to get in touch with anyone who lived there in the past, or even anybody who knew anybody who lived there and had problems."

And so the case of the State College duplex was closed. As is so often the case with paranormal investigations, though, it has hardly been resolved. Maybe Patty will get a call when another attractive Penn State student with psychic tendencies moves in. Until then, the PGRF founder hopes the ghost of Thomas Glenn will keep his distance from, and his hands off, the lovely college coeds.

3
Unsolved Mysteries

Evergreen Cemetery

As long as he can remember, Bill Washell has been interested in the supernatural. Attributing his life-long love to
the horror movies he watched as a child, Bill says his passion for the ghoulish eventually developed into a fascination with the afterlife, which sent him tramping through
cemeteries and haunted houses on the lookout for any
real-life evidence of its existence. Bill was already a com-
mitted ghost hunter when he moved from South Carolina
to Maine in the late 1990s. Not long after he settled down
in Lewiston, Bill decided that he'd chosen the best possible place for a paranormal enthusiast to live. And it didn't
really have anything to do with the fact that Maine was
the home state of his favorite author, the master of
macabre literature, Stephen King.

It was the ghosts. There were hauntings in Maine—
lots of them. From its middle-American towns and cities,
to the rocky promontories of the eastern coastline, to the
dark shadows of its wooded interior, Maine was full of
supernatural folklore. Bill isn't able to say why the state
has such a wealth of ghostly tales, but it does make perfect
sense to him that the most prolific horror writer in the
world lived there. There is no shortage of inspiration.

Bill himself has received no shortage of inspiration
from Maine's paranormal landscape. He established
Maine's Paranormal Research Association (MPRA) in
1998 with two goals in mind: 1) to find and investigate
ghosts and hauntings with the hope of acquiring a better
understanding of paranormal phenomenon, and 2) aiding individuals with difficulties dealing with these same

phenomena. His group doesn't aim to get rid of ghosts. Rather than confront spirits, the MPRA opts to educate people who find themselves face to face with the paranormal. According to their mission statement, "the MPRA will educate (its) clients and the public as to the true nature of their situation and assist them with dealing with these spirits on a daily basis. If (it) is unable to fulfill this, (it) will work with the client to find someone who can assist them properly." According to Bill's experiences, people come to the MPRA wanting confirmation rather than exorcisms. "Most of the people who contact us just need to be told that they aren't losing their minds," Bill says. "They want to be told that this kind of stuff does happen, and there are *some* explanations."

The MPRA keeps busy. When the group isn't being called on to investigate haunted houses, members turn their attention to any one of the many cemeteries in Maine said to be haunted. Including houses and cemeteries, the MPRA has averaged 20 to 35 cases a year since 1998, but its signature investigation site is a cemetery called Evergreen.

"Evergreen Cemetery was built in 1855," Bill begins. "It's a historical landmark, designated by the National Historical Society. At 235 acres, it's the biggest cemetery in Maine, and a lot of prominent people are buried there." Over the years, the sprawling burial ground has been the site of countless bizarre happenings. There have been so many inexplicable phenomena said to have occurred there—wandering apparitions, whispering tombstones, cold spots, flashing lights in the middle of the night—that the cemetery is part of the local folklore. Popular as

Evergreen Cemetery is a favorite site among paranormal enthusiasts in Maine.

Evergreen is among paranormal enthusiasts and folk-lorists, interest in the cemetery traditionally peaks on Halloween when the local news channels features the cemetery for their obligatory spook-themed segments. That's how the members of Bill's ghost-hunting group came to conduct their first investigation there.

"We were introduced to Evergreen in Halloween of 2002 by a radio crew," Bill says. "They wanted us to walk through and see if we picked up anything." Though their findings their first time out weren't too dramatic, the cold spots, EVP and numerous orbs that came up in their photographs were enough to convince Bill's crew that the site was would be worth future investigations. It became the MPRA's pet project.

During the next two years, whenever there was a lull between cases, Bill's group headed off to Evergreen for another look. Every time they went, their findings were always interesting enough to warrant further investigation. They found all the usual temperature variations, EVP and photographs that captured all sorts of orbs and ectoplasmic mists. Nothing too dramatic, to be sure, but always enough to keep Bill's crew interested, and certainly enough to justify the cemetery's reputation. Given all the anomalies that occurred, it seemed as if Evergreen was truly crawling with entities existing beyond the mortal pale. Nevertheless, it took nearly two years of observations, EMF and photography for Bill Washell and his group of ghost hunters to actually see one of the spirits of Evergreen.

In September 2004, the MPRA members were going about their Evergreen investigation just as they had so many times before. With audio recorders running, cameras and infrared thermometers at hand, they separated into pairs and spread out over the cemetery. Bill was partnered with a fellow investigator, Stacy. "We were walking near one of the corners of the cemeteries when we noticed movement coming from about 50 feet in front of us," Bill says. Stacy let out a startled gasp at the very same moment Bill noticed it.

From 50 feet away, all they were able to discern was movement in the darkness, but the ghost hunters had instant suspicions. At that moment, the readings on their Tri-Field EMF meters began to jump. Then, in the next moment, it was there. "We both looked up from our Tri-Fields and there was a white figure standing between two tombstones ahead of us," Bill says. Steeling their courage, Bill and Stacy began advancing towards the figure. "At about 20 feet, we could see that it was a woman dressed in white," Bill continues. "But we wouldn't get a closer look because just when I was about to snap a picture, she disappeared right in front of us."

Without warning—just like that, the Lady in White vanished. Neither Bill nor Stacy were able to make out any details of her appearance; only that she was a woman with long hair and was clothed in white. "We weren't quick enough to get a photograph of her," Bill says, "but we snapped quite a few shots of where she was standing when she disappeared." And what did these photos turn up?

"The first picture turned up black," Bill says, "like someone had put a hand up over the camera lens. The second photograph was of me standing where she was, and we got some anomalies on that one." The "anomalies" that Bill refers to are the orbs and ectoplasmic mists that are commonly accepted among ghost hunters as evidence of ghostly activity.

Of all the different types of evidence ghost hunters stumble upon during their investigations, apparitions such as the one Bill and Stacy spotted are the rarest and most sought-after, and Bill is hardly nonchalant about what he saw that night. "No matter how long you've been doing this," the veteran investigator says, "there's nothing like the feeling you get when you spot a full-body apparition." At the time of this writing, Bill Washell had only ever spotted such an entity a few times before, and he describes the experience as a combination of fear, fascination and awe.

Very little is known about Evergreen's Lady in White. "The only thing we've come up with is that she might have been a student at the local college," Bill says. Or so goes the local legend, according to one of Bill's field investigators. But given the fact that all the MPRA's research since the sighting has turned up nothing to corroborate the story, it seems as if this dead student might be nothing more than an urban legend.

That said, Bill is certain of what he and Stacy saw, and they aren't the only ones. The Lady in White is one of Evergreen cemetery's most frequently sighted spirits. While locals may have made up the tale of the dead college student to explain the apparition, the fact that such a story was even invented lends some weight to her existence. Though no one is definitely sure who she is or why she continues to appear, locals are more than certain that she is actually there. After September 2004, count Bill Washell and the MPRA among the believers.

Needless to say, the MPRA will return to Evergreen. Even if there is a shortage of solid explanations for why the ghosts haunt the cemetery (that is, besides the immediate presence of so many buried dead), its prior experience of supernatural phenomena is enough to encourage the MPRA to continue. And who knows? One of these days they may actually communicate with one of the many spirits said to haunt Evergreen. Is it only a matter of time before MPRA's audio recorders pick up a woman's voice from the Lady in White's corner of the cemetery? Could Washell's next foray into the enormous Maine burial ground uncover the ghost's long-standing mystery? If so, the MPRA need not worry; by all accounts, there are many other ghosts to hound in Evergreen.

The First Man Buried in Alta Loma

It's been said that Richard Smith is something of a recluse who, as a rule, avoids interviews with snooping writers. "I'm too busy doin' my own interviews," the native Texan quips, referring to his practically constant search for EVP wherever he is, day or night. But the funny thing about Rich is that as difficult as it was to corner him into a conversation, once he got started on the subject of paranormal investigation, there was no stopping him.

If there's one thing that ought to be said about Rich's ghost-hunting methods, it's that he takes EVP very, very seriously. So seriously, in fact, that he's known to carry a wire on him day to day, just in case a ghost happens upon him when he isn't expecting it. According to Smith, ghosts are all around us, and so in a sense it follows that the dedicated ghost hunter should always be on the hunt. That this dedicated ghost hunter from the Houston–Galveston area has gravitated to EVP as his primary method of investigation is no surprise, given his background.

A volunteer for the navy during the Vietnam War, Richard enrolled in a naval aviation training facility and excelled so well in his courses that he was quickly moved into a secret Naval Intelligence spy plane squadron. During his duty with the navy, he specialized in electronics warfare, earned his crewman wings as an electronics intelligence equipment operator and flew over 100 missions.

Quick to make use of these skills in civilian life after his stint in the navy, Rich worked for a while in industrial electronics. But it wasn't until he coupled his electronic talents with his fascination with the paranormal that Rich found his true calling. Today, Rich is probably one of the most knowledgeable EVP men around. He is the founder of Paranormal Investigations of Texas—a two-person outfit consisting of him and his partner, Mary—and has written a book on the subject of ghosts and EVP. *Everywhere I See Ghosts* is a chronicle of his and Mary's constant search for the things that go bump in the night...or, rather, go boo! in his recorder.

One such tale involving a long-dead cowboy and the historic Alta Loma cemetery in Galveston occurred during the winter of 2001. The small town of Alta Loma was actually quite close to where the couple lived, but they had never bothered investigating it before because they hadn't realized how old it was. Their first visit was a short one. As Rich puts it: "We were wondering if the local folks in this small town might not take well to a couple of strangers wandering around their cemetery with cameras, electronics measuring devices and recording apparatus." So, just to play safe, they decided to make the investigation short and to the point.

They arrived at the cemetery about an hour before sunset on a clear, pleasant night. According to their investigative routine, Mary and Rich each pulled out their recorders and headed off in opposite directions with tapes running, on the hunt for EVP. Along with his recorder, Rich had his EMF meter out, scanning for fluctuations in the electromagnetic field. "I noticed right away that my electrical field measuring devices were indicating a higher than normal ambient reading of magnetic fields in the area," Rich begins. "The readings at this moment were not necessarily typical of ghostly activity, and I suspected a man-made source."

Sure enough, Rich's suspicions were on the nose. His EMF meter led him straight to the edge of the cemetery, where a row of electrical poles was feeding wires to nearby homes. So much for the EMF readings; the spike in the magnetic field was being caused by these power lines, not by any paranormal energies present in the cemetery. Yet though localized fluctuations in the electromagnetic field are common indicators of supernatural activity, Rich knew that they weren't the only indicator, and he continued through the cemetery.

For Rich, this row of electrical lines was the closest thing to a ghost he encountered that night. After registering nada in ghosts, he was surprised to see Mary standing there with a smile on her face. Mary had a bit more luck. She'd gotten one.

At first, Rich could barely believe his ears when he played back the recording. He'd heard a lot of strange things on EVP tapes, but this message was one of the strangest.

"Yee haw?" Rich looked at Mary in bewilderment. "He said 'yee haw?' " Actually, contrary to the true Texan tradition, the voice actually hadn't said or shouted "yee haw." The "yee haw" came across as a whisper. The spirit had whispered it right in Mary's ear.

Mary smiled again. "He likes me," was all she said.

Given Mary's past experiences with EVP, it seems as if a number of spirits have taken a liking to her. Richard explains: "Thus far, approximately 75 percent of Mary's

EVP recordings come up as whispers. Generally speaking, the nature of her recordings has been messages of relative calm, peace and thoughtful contemplation." Rich's experiences, on the other hand, have been markedly different. Frequently recording swearing voices and angry retorts among generally pleasant messages, Rich apparently has a way of bringing out the bitterness in certain spirits.

The ghost hunter has a theory: "At this point we have no proven explanation for the peaceful nature of Mary's EVP experiences except to say that Mary is inwardly the most gentle and sweet person I've known. And many people who study the paranormal, myself included, firmly believe that when emotional and mental energies are released to the spiritual plane, they have a tendency to receive similar energies in return. In other words, if you transmit fear or anger when communicating with the spirit planes, then you must be prepared to attract the same in return." Which leads Rich to wisely conclude that anyone planning communicate with spirits would do well to "purge" any negative emotions before making the attempt.

Later that night the couple was going over the evidence they collected. Besides Mary's "yee haw" EVP, they'd come up dry. While it isn't rare for ghost hunters to get skunked on an investigation, Rich is something of an expert at getting in touch with spirits. For him to come out without a single EVP is very unusual. Yet curious as Rich was by this result, subsequent events that night would prove that the haunting at Alta Loma was no run-of-the-mill affair.

Hours later, in the small hours of the morning, Mary was woken from a deep sleep and saw, through half-closed eyes, a man standing in the doorway. The man looked like

he could have been in his late 20s. He had dark hair, cowboy boots, a flannel shirt and plain pants. He looked at
Mary before he spoke. "I was murdered," he said, as
calmly and matter-of-factly as someone commenting on
the weather. And then he vanished, right before Mary's
eyes. Mary was astounded. Even as she settled back to
sleep, she somehow knew beyond any doubt that this
apparition was the man she'd heard in the cemetery. The
whispering cowboy had followed her home.

It was the first thing on her mind when she woke up in
the morning. During the morning's bustle, as she was seeing Rich and her kids off to work and school, she wondered if the spirit was still there, hovering unseen in their
home. Rich didn't seem to be able to sense it, and she
didn't think now was the time to tell him about it. Maybe
it was all in her imagination. Could it have been a dream?

Alone now, she sat on the front porch, unable to think
about anything but the cowboy. It was his words—"I was
murdered." She kept repeating them in her mind. It
seemed to be all she could think of, and she couldn't figure out why. Then she realized *she* wasn't repeating them,
they were being repeated to her. All at once it dawned on
her. The ghost of the cowboy was speaking to her right
then and there. He'd followed her and Rich back from the
cemetery, and he was in their home. "Listen to me," he
seemed to be saying now, though Mary wasn't so much
hearing the words as she was feeling them. Eager to hear
what this spirit wanted to say, Mary grabbed her digital
recorder.

It's common knowledge among ghost hunters that
spirit voices often lost on human ears come up as EVP on

recording devices. This supernatural theory is definitely one of the stranger ones. Seriously, how can sound recorders pick up inaudible sounds?

Rich Smith explains: "One of the first pieces of equipment a paranormal investigator will acquire is a 'magnetic field detector' or field measuring device. Aberrations in magnetic fields occur in many documented paranormal events."

Whatever it is about ghosts and the electromagnetic field, it is possible that audio recorders pick up EVP. That's the idea. "Essentially, the recorder is a device that uses a low-level magnetic field, thus magnetic field changes may be found on the recording device," Rich says. The theory is that the EVP makes its way onto recording devices via these magnetic disturbances rather than microphones, which are unable to pick up any of the inaudible words the ghosts may be uttering.

That is why Mary, fully aware of this theory, rushed for her recorder. For all she knew, the cowboy could have been singing "The Ballad of Sam Bass," and she wouldn't have heard a word. With her recorder running, Mary began asking questions out loud. "It's okay for you to talk to me," she said. "Tell me what's on your mind."

Because the cowboy's presence seemed strongest when she'd been outside on the porch, she walked out onto the front lawn. As she walked silently back and forth across the yard, taking in every sound of that Texan morning, she was once again aware of the spirit's presence. She wasn't so much hearing his thoughts as she was sensing what he was feeling. And she was picking up on one thing and one thing only—frustration.

When Rich got back home from work, Mary told him of her EVP investigation that morning. "We were both anxious to hear the EVP," Rich says. "So we took the first opportunity to load the audio into our extensive computer lab in the house for analysis." Extensive computer lab is right. By Rich's description, Paranormal Investigations of Texas' audio room sounds like a ghost hunter's bat cave. "Two separate computer lab set-ups with multiple audio filtering and analysis systems take up an entire 16-foot wall in the house."

It often takes a good deal of audio tweaking and software manipulation to find the EVP buried in digital recordings. That was definitely the case with the cowboy's EVP. Mary looked on as Rich adjusted and readjusted his electric gadgetry, looking for some sort of voice in the five-minute recording. Finally, after they'd been there for nearly an hour, a voice began to emerge from the audio file.

It was a man's voice, repeating the same words over and over in a strange, frustrated whisper: "number…the numbers…it's the numbers." Gone was the flirtatious "yee haw" of the day before. There was nothing pleased or playful here. This voice was that of a man obsessed with something that was frustrating him to no end. The hushed voice kept up the "numbers" mantra for a few minutes before fading away.

"What on earth did this cryptic message mean?" Rich wonders. "Were we hearing clues to the frustration of a spirit who was forced to exit this life before his time?" Rich and Mary were stumped. The ghost hunters had no idea, but Mary was set on getting to the bottom of this mystery, insisting that she and Rich depart immediately for another investigation at the cemetery. Rich was never one to put the brakes on a ghost hunt, but this time he had to make an exception.

He explains, "You see, Mary had been experiencing some very distressing health problems. It had only recently been learned that Mary's heart murmur, which she had for years, had suddenly begun to get worse. A major valve in her heart was failing and she was growing weaker and would soon be scheduled for a critical surgery."

Given her current state of health, Rich was hesitant to go off to communicate with a potentially traumatized ghost. "I felt that an intense encounter with an entity bearing a message about murder and possible intrigue should be avoided in order to prevent undue pressure and anxiety for Mary," Rich says. "So with a little pressure from myself, Mary agreed to curtail this rather scary scenario until she regained her strength."

That was back in the winter of 2001. Mary has since had the surgery to replace the failing valve in her heart, and has recovered nicely. Nevertheless, the pair of ghost hunters has yet to go back to the Alta Loma Cemetery for a follow-up. So the mystery of "the numbers" remains unsolved. One can hardly blame Rich for not going back for a second visit, though. After all, how many ghost hunters would be eager to go after a spirit that had taken a liking to their loved one? All things considered, the buried cowboy might have to wait a while before he gets his message across about "the numbers."

The Tamaqua Elks Club

The small town of Tamaqua lies on the U.S. 209, near the northeast border of Schulykill County. Once a center for the booming anthracite industry that dominated the region, Tamaqua has since settled into peaceful repose— another small Pennsylvania town in the verdant countryside. But Tamaqua has not faded into obscurity. One of the town's buildings has attracted the attention of paranormal enthusiasts, bringing people from all across the state to the doorstep of the local Elks Club building, seeking access to the old structure's famous third floor.

Built in the 1800s, the stone edifice is one of Tamaqua's oldest standing buildings. It was purchased by the Elks Club in 1906, and has served as a tavern, restaurant and meeting area for the local Elks. With a bar on the first floor, a dining room and meeting hall on the second, and boarding rooms and a ballroom on the third, there was more than enough business coming in to keep the Elks' building afloat.

Nothing unusual occurred within the walls of the Elks' Tamaqua headquarters for decades, until a string of deaths on the third floor cast a dark shadow over the whole floor. The first casualty was discovered early one morning years ago, when waking early-birds found one of the boarders hanging by her neck from the staircase banister on the third floor. All evidence led to the conclusion that the woman had taken her own life. Although no one knows for certain what drove her to do such a horrible thing, succeeding events suggest that her motivation may have been family related. A few years later, this woman's brother decided on a disturbingly similar course of action. After checking into the Elks Club for an evening, he was found the next morning dangling at the end of rope tied to his doorframe.

The fact that the two suicides took place in the same building was enough to get people talking. When it became known that they were brother and sister, people began attaching bizarre stories to the third floor. Everyone knew someone who knew somebody who heard footsteps in the hallway when no one was there. Others spoke of doors slamming shut or opening bereft of any visible physical force. There were also reports of inexplicable cold spells that could convert a comfortable room into a meat locker within a few short minutes, only to gradually warm up again for no discernable reason.

The tenor of these stories changed after 1970, when another person was found dead in one of the boarding rooms. Though this man died of natural causes, probably expiring peacefully in his sleep, things on the third floor took a marked turn shortly after his passing. Whereas before, stories about the Elks Club's top floor were tinged with the whimsy of any tall tale, guests' accounts grew ever more frequent and darker after the last man passed on. People spoke of the new chill that permeated the air there—a strange kind of heaviness that hung in the ether, blanketing all light in a thin filter, deepening shadows and smothering light. The previously fanciful tales about the building were transformed into individuals' terrifying experiences.

One man walking to his room late in the evening was confronted by what he would later describe as a humanoid shadow, a black, featureless shape moving down the hall toward him. The man could only stand speechless as the figure passed right through his body, leaving him shivering in the cold and unable to breath as it continued past. The experience was so traumatic that he packed up his things and left that night, never to return. Another boarder spent an entire evening lying fearfully in bed, fixated on a dark corner in his room. He could see nothing there but swore that some sort of malevolent presence was silently looming there, staring at him with hatred. Too scared to fall asleep, too scared to move, the man left the Elks Club at first light; he never went up to the third floor again.

Then there is the story of the lone plumber who was working in one of the rooms. He was inspecting a pipe that ran behind the walls when the door to the room slammed violently shut behind him. Puzzled and a little startled, the man walked across the room to open the door, only to discover that it had been locked. More angry than frightened, the plumber began banging on the door, yelling at whoever had locked him in to let him out. About 10 minutes went by before he heard the latch click open. A loud rebuke was already halfway out his lips as he swung the door open, but he fell into a shocked silence when he stepped into the darkened, completely deserted hallway. There was no one there. He realized that there was no way anyone could have disappeared down the hallway that quickly, so he turned back to his work. He finished as quickly as he could in the suddenly foreboding room, then bolted down to the main floor—another man who promised himself never to venture up the Elks Club's stairs again.

Stories such as these circulated through Tamaqua and beyond, branding the Elks Club meeting hall as one of the county's haunted sites. A very real fear of the boarding rooms took root among the visitors to the Elks Club, and business on the third floor began to whittle away. The rooms were finally shut down after 1970. The only people who venture to the top floor today are reluctant Elks employees whose work duties take them there, or paranormal investigators actively seeking some kind of encounter with the denizens of the afterworld. For several years now, the spirits in the Elks Club have come under the scrutiny of a multitude of psychics and ghost hunters, whose findings have done nothing but confirm the local stories about the Elks' meeting hall. Seldom do those who venture to Tamaqua for paranormal purposes leave the building disappointed.

Almost every kind of supernatural indicator that paranormal investigators are able to detect has been recorded in the Elks building at one time or another. Glowing circles of light that appear on photographs of haunted locations—referred to as "orbs" by ghost hunters, they are thought to be celluloid representations of ghosts—have turned up in droves in the photographs taken on the Elks Club third floor. In addition to photographs riddled with inexplicable pinpoints of light, ghost hunters have recorded completely unaccountable drops in temperature. There have been occasions when psychics have been grabbed by ice-cold hands that seem to have come out of the very walls. Others have had terrifying visions of figures cloaked in flame, roaring at them to get off the third floor. Every one of these experiences has been recorded by different paranormal societies, adding to the substantial store of supernatural accounts about the Elks Club building.

A local ghost hunter named Sean Snyder has done some of his own research on the third floor, adding his experiences there to the ever-waxing body of accounts about the site. After arriving in Tamaqua early in November 2001, the young ghost enthusiast set up for what was to be one of his most dramatic investigations.

All the findings were documented with digital equipment. Snyder began with photographs of the enigmatic bloodstain located beneath the banister of the third-floor stairs, just under the area where the woman hanged herself so many years ago. The owners have painted over the reddish-brown mark several times, but no matter how thick the coat of paint, the stain continues to reappear as a reminder of one woman's miserable demise at the end of a rope. That was just the beginning.

"There really was a lot of supernatural activity there," Snyder recalls today. "We took 22 pictures with orbs in them." The shots were taken whenever the photographer felt anything was unusual. If he was struck by sudden chills while standing in a room, Snyder would point and click at the air around him. Most of these photos yielded orbs hovering all around, invisible to the naked eye but somehow registering on celluloid. "My father arrived near the end of the investigation," Snyder recalls. "He was standing in one of the rooms when he was hit by this weird sensation that the ground was going beneath him."

When Sean's father told him what he was feeling, the ghost investigator snapped a shot of his dad. Sure enough, the photograph revealed the presence of a large orb hovering just above his father's head.

Sean's findings were not limited to stationary orbs in still photographs. He also caught six moving orbs on video camera. These entities, invisible to the naked eye as well, appear on video as streaking balls of light, moving quickly across the picture. There is no single theory explaining what these moving lights are, but some investigators have dramatic footage of these orbs colliding with the people filming them. And though they are not seen without the aid of a video camera, they are definitely felt, for people have been jarred, startled or profoundly terrified when they have felt the sudden impact of a moving orb.

There is one corner on the third floor where other groups have had fairly intense supernatural experiences. It is always in the same corner of the same room: some groups have been suddenly seized by the undeniable feeling that someone or something was standing right beside them. In this spot, one psychic felt a frigid hand come through the wall and grab her, and a terrifying flaming figure appeared to sensitive mediums, demanding they leave the room immediately. Snyder was standing in this room when the temperature suddenly plummeted and all of his recording equipment cut out on him. There was no reasonable explanation. Not even a trace of a draft whispered through the room, and all the batteries in his equipment were fresh. "It only lasted for a couple of seconds,"

Sean remembers, "and then the temperature went back to normal and all the equipment just turned on again."

There one moment, gone the next, whatever force was acting in that corner left no explanation for its visitation, leaving Sean wondering what had just happened and why. The erratic jumps of his EMF meter did not help at all. While it was obvious that something was disrupting the electromagnetic field on the third floor, any guesses at what these forces actually were are just that: guesses.

Like all the paranormal societies that were in Tamaqua before him, Sean Snyder took notes on his investigation, filing them away with all his other explorations in eastern Pennsylvania. The nature of these reports is similar to those of many paranormal societies across the country— they exhibit an overabundance of empirical observation and a rather conspicuous shortage of sound explanations. The suicides that took place on the third floor seem to have something to do with the bizarre goings-on in the Elks Club building, but there is no way of knowing how or why these spirits remain behind. While neither Sean Snyder nor any other ghost hunter can claim to have the definitive explanation, it may be said that nothing less than the mysteries of the afterlife are locked within such hauntings as those in the Tamaqua building. And as long as questions of life, death and the soul remain mysteries to humanity, the proprietors of the Elks Club should continue to expect visitors interested in looking through the third floor.

The Anonymous
Ghost Hunters

No book on ghost hunters would be complete without coming to grips with one central issue. Up until now, this book has ducked this issue, sidestepped it, ignored it—but no more. It's time to meet it head on. "What issue is this?" you may ask.

C'mon. It's the stigma. It's the popular stigma that goes along with—has always gone along with—paranormal investigation.

Never mind that a person who merely entertains a belief in ghosts risks defying the overriding rationalism of our time. What about those people who not only believe but go out of their way to "hunt" ghosts? There's no shortage of descriptors that skeptics may apply: quacks, loons, weirdoes, charlatans. Of course, such virulent reactions are nothing new.

The opening pages of this book chronicle the popular reaction to Emmanuel Swedenborg when he gave up a distinguished career in science and pronounced that he was able to talk to dead people. Promptly denounced by the same scientific community that once held him in high regard, Swedenborg lived the rest of his life enduring the snickers and sneers of his former peers. Decades later, when the Spiritualist movement spread through the United States and Britain, and it seemed that everyone knew someone who had psychic gifts, a group of debunkers arose to counter the claims of self-styled psychics. Some of these debunkers grew to be more famous than the psychics they debunked. Harry Houdini, one such naysayer, employed his own mastery of stage magic and sleight-of-hand to expose fraudulent psychic performers.

It was Spiritualism and the claims of psychics that impelled the formation of the Society for Psychical Research (SPR) in the late 19th century. From the onset, this organization existed to examine the psychic phenomena that were spreading across nations on both sides of the Atlantic. Though the SPR counted among its members such eminent scientists and men of letters as Sir William Crookes, Sigmund Freud, Sir Arthur Conan Doyle and Carl Jung, those who joined the society risked ostracization from mainstream science. The venerated William Crookes experienced this contempt first-hand when early investigations led him to believe in the existence of psychic forces. Believing this newly discovered phenomenon to be of primary scientific importance, Crookes wrote a paper on the subject and submitted it to the Royal Society for publication. The august organization refused to print the article, and though Crookes eventually got it published in the *Journal of Quarterly Science*, the furor the article caused resulted in Crookes' ultimate split from the scientific community. No one even bothered to subject his findings to experimentation. "Never mind his findings!" the intellects may have piped up. "The mere fact that he'd gone out and done the research was enough to cast him into suspicion."

Ever since this first wave of near knee-jerk skepticism from the scientific community, paranormal investigation has been pushed to the fringes of human endeavor. From famous investigators such as Harry Price to all the lesser-known groups that post their findings on the Internet today, ghost hunters are regarded with more than a little doubt by the general population.

It makes sense, then, that some investigators out there today would prefer to keep their identities secret. Ghost hunters are intrigued by the afterlife—the idea of spirits that remain on earth after death. They also have faith enough in human faculties to believe that questions of spirits and the afterlife might be answered through investigation and analysis. However, not all of them are eager to have their names attached to their investigations.

The desire for anonymity is definitely an anomaly in the subculture of paranormal investigation. Most ghost hunters want to get their names out there. In the eyes of many investigators, success is measured by fame, and fame is invariably measured by the discovery of new hauntings, with spectacular findings. For others, it isn't fame, but the thrill of investigation and the satisfaction of discovery. These ghost hunters usually value their findings enough to post them in a public space (usually the Internet), so that anyone who's interested can get more information. Yet while anonymous ghost hunters might shun any recognition for their activities, they aren't entirely immune to the thrill of investigation and the satisfaction of discovery. Or else why would they go out of their way to get their stories told in this book? Anonymous ghost hunters want their stories told; they just don't want to deal with the stigma that accompanies their peculiar hobby. These following two accounts deal with such investigators who obviously want to get their incredible experiences out, but have no wish to be ostracized for doing it. We shall respect their wishes.

Mr. Bigby

"John Davies," as our first anonymous ghost hunter shall be called for this story, keeps his paranormal pastime secret. "If you knew the type of people I associate with, you'd understand," Davies says. "Everyone, from my work associates to my family—if they knew I was into this stuff, they'd be real concerned."

Concerned about what?

"Well, for starters, my work is definitely high responsibility. There's a lot riding on my shoulders, and my clients, if that's what you want to call them, really put a lot of faith in my ability to think straight, rationally and quickly. Trust me when I say that a lot of them wouldn't be too thrilled to know that I chase ghosts around. There's a certain conduct expected in my profession, and ghost hunting would definitely go against it. I can't think of anyone I work with who would be understanding. As for my family—my family would just worry. So I keep it to myself."

John doesn't get into specifics about what he does, but that's not important for the story. What's more interesting is why he would bother with ghost hunting if it is in such staunch opposition to his professional values?

"Well, for me, it has to do with something I experienced when I was young." John pauses for a moment before continuing. "I hope this isn't going to sound too Hollywood, but it probably will. My mother passed on when I was young. None of us knew it growing up, but she was born with a congenital heart condition, and extreme fibrillation took her life when she was in her early 40s."

His mother had departed without even saying good-bye, and no one could give him a satisfactory answer about what was going on. Understandably, John began to obsess about his mother. "My brothers and I understood that our father didn't want to talk about it. It was written all over him. And of course, this wasn't the kind of thing you discussed with friends at that age."

Without anyone to turn to, night after night, after the lights had been turned off and he'd been tucked in, John began speaking into the darkness and incredibly, the darkness spoke back to him. "I'm not sure how it started, and if I really knew what was going on."

But every night, the voice that John was having his nightly conversations with seemed to become more real. When it began, the voice sounded cold, far away. Sometimes John's young ears weren't able to make out what exactly it was saying. With each passing evening, the voice sounded clearer, more distinct. John remembers, "One night, I was speaking with a lady who seemed to really like me and want the best for me. And I realized that she was my mother."

And what did John have to say to the spirit of his departed mother? "First I asked her where she was, and in my room, from the area around my chair, I heard her voice say: 'Someplace nice.' Then I asked her why she had to go. 'Because it was my time to go,' she said to me. 'When it's our time, we all have to go.' I remember that really scared me. I remember saying I didn't want to go, and then I remember feeling bad about saying this because she'd already gone." John explains.

"I told you this might sound too Hollywood, or maybe too crazy would be a better way to put it. But I believe it to this day: my mother came back to say good-bye. In my memory, she was in this dim blue light, almost like moonlight. I can't remember anything but her face and her hands. And they were the same as they always were. She told me everything was going to be okay, she touched my face and then she was gone. She never came back to speak with me again."

This is John's story. There are those who will have their doubts. John himself recognizes the issues. "I know, I know," the ghost hunter says. "People are going to be skeptical. And who knows? Maybe they ought to be. A young child sees a recently departed parent who puts his mind at ease about death and then vanishes? People are going to say I dreamed it up. Kids and their overactive imaginations, right? There is a psychological explanation: 'I was dealing with extreme stress, and my mind created the vision of my mother as a coping mechanism.' I'm sure that's what some people will say."

Yet even as the months turned to years and into decades, John never forgot the vision of his mother's spirit. He wasn't haunted by it, or tormented. Sometimes entire months would go by without him thinking about it, but the memory would always return—the spirit of mother, back for just a few minutes to comfort her son. "By the time I was in college, the questions really started popping. I began to wonder about other people who'd died. Was everyone able to come back and communicate with their loved ones? If that was the case, why didn't it happen more often? Imagine all the heartache that would be spared if more dead people came back to tell their sons and daughters and husbands and wives that everything was okay.

"There was only so much time I could spend asking myself those questions before I started trying to find my own answers," John says. "My way to those answers has been the only way I've known throughout my professional career—through science."

Hence John's preoccupation with paranormal investigation began. In a way, then, John's been looking for his mother ever since he went out to investigate his first haunted site.

John found out about the house in Cleveland on a web site. Taking great pains to keep his ghost-hunting activities secret, John never explores hauntings in his hometown, but makes sure that every investigation he conducts is in another part of the country. "Some people might say this is going too far, but what can I say? I'm protective of my privacy, and anyway," John laughs, "I'm an inveterate bachelor; what else am I going to do for holidays?"

Well, lucky for John there are web sites that allow people to post their own experiences with ghosts. Through the last few years, it's been an invaluable resource for the cautious ghost hunter, allowing him to set up investigations with people across the country over the Internet, thereby keeping his identity secret. Some of these web sites, like Shadowlands (theshadowlands.net/ghost/) have thousands of entries. Before such web sites as Shadowlands, John's investigations were mostly limited to well-known hauntings in public places such as cemeteries, museums, churches and the like. Not anymore.

"Well, I was corresponding with the old lady who lived in this Cleveland home for the better part of a month before I decided that this was going to be my next investigation. It was in the spring of 1999, and I booked a full week off work for the trip to Ohio," John says. "I actually made the decision to visit this woman's home after her first e-mail. She was a perfect candidate; activity in her home was common enough that I stood a good chance of catching something while I was there. Also, her e-mails were smart and she seemed like a decent lady, not the type of person who would make up these kinds of stories."

While John keeps the woman's name and address to himself, he's free with the details. "She was an old woman, just over 70, who was recently widowed and living alone in a big old Cleveland home," the ghost hunter begins. "She told me in her first missive that she'd known her house was haunted for years, but she'd never really talked to anyone about it." John relates. It sounded like typical paranormal activity for the most part. The usual: things would go missing and reappear days later in weird places. In some spots of the house, the temperature would drop sharply and then go back to normal in a matter of seconds."

Over the years, the ghost had always appeared in the same room, and always in the same fashion. Preceded by a swirling haze of light silvery mist that formed in the small study on the second floor, a semi-transparent old man would appear in the corner of the room, stand there for several minutes, and then vanish as quickly as he came. The woman had seen him countless times. She was able to recall his appearance to the smallest detail—the silver

Preceded by a light silvery mist, a semi-transparent old man would appear in the corner of the small study.

hair, bushy sideburns and droopy moustache; the hunched shoulders, the somber stare.

John goes on to say that the woman believed the spirit had always given her special attention. While her children might casually mention footsteps they'd heard every few months, she'd hear these same footsteps every other week. If her husband complained about a missing tie or tool once or twice a year, the woman was losing things far more frequently. While the rest of the family never considered that their home might be haunted, she found herself face-to-face with this ghost several times a year. "One of the reasons, perhaps, that she was the only person who ever saw the ghost was because she was the only who spent any time in that room," John says.

The family understood that the study was her corner of the house, and she was very rarely bothered when she shut the door and settled in with a book. Except, of course, when the old man would appear in the corner. "What puzzled me about this woman was that, in all those years, when she knew that there was this ghost in her house, she never said a word about it!" John says. "I only asked her about this once, the first day I met her face-to-face at her house."

John laughs when he recalls her response. "She just looked at me with this mischievous smile. I think she said something like: 'I thought it was rather nice. It was my own little secret. A woman's allowed a secret or two, isn't she?' All right, I thought. Fair enough."

Evidently, this woman wasn't frightened of the ghost. Indeed, over the years, she seems to have even learned to take some comfort from it. After all, it was the one thing that remained constant, the one thing she could rely on to stay the same. Her husband died and her kids grew up and moved away, but the old man was always there, appearing in the same corner every time, surrounded by silvery mist, standing there with that same impassive stare.

Then things began to change, and when they did, the solitary woman living in the big old house wasn't sure what to make of it. She was unable to tell John when the changes began, exactly. They began gradually; at first, she thought nothing of them, thinking that she may have been imagining them. The disembodied footsteps in the second-floor hallway that she'd become accustomed to years and years ago were not so gentle and plodding anymore. Every time she heard them, they seemed to be getting louder, faster. Where once they seemed to shuffle, now they strode boldly down the hall, stopping always right at her bedroom door. Not only was this nocturnal walk getting louder, it was also occurring more often.

The ghost also seemed to be acquiring quicker hands. Her belongings had never exactly been safe in the house; a purse she'd put away in a closet would inexplicably vanish, then appear a few days later in the basement, or a book that she'd last seen on a tabletop turned up in the laundry hamper. It was one of things she'd learn to put up with, but by the time she was corresponding with John, the thieving had become a less of a nuisance and more of a problem. Her things were now being stolen almost every day.

But most alarming was the apparition itself, or "Mr. Bigby," as she'd taken to calling him long ago. The Mr. Bigby she knew had always been pleasant enough: quietly appearing, remaining for no more than a few minutes and then vanishing without a word. The ghost now seemed to have acquired some unsettling new habits.

She'd practically jumped out of her chair the first time it dawned on her that the ghost was actually looking at her. It had occurred in early December of the previous year. She was in her study reading a book in her favorite chair when Mr. Bigby appeared in the corner of the room, like he had countless times before, but for the first time in decades, the ghost in the corner was looking straight at her. No, he was looking straight through her. Something about the look shook her up terribly. Why, after years of staring blankly ahead, had Mr. Bigby shifted his gaze? Mr. Bigby began appearing with unnerving frequency from then on, his eyes fixed on her in a blood-chilling gaze every time.

Yet she wouldn't leave the study. The room had been hers for decades, and she wasn't about to let Mr. Bigby chase her out. Until he spoke to her, that is. It happened on a dark February evening. The ghost was appearing at least once a week at that point, so when he shimmered into sight, the woman did her best to ignore the eyes she knew were fixed on her.

"I'm not looking at you, Mr. Bigby," the old woman spoke aloud. "So you can forget about giving me those creepy eyes."

When she told John about Mr. Bigby's response, she talked about the *sound*. There were no words, just a *sound*—a low guttural moan that made her drop her book and get out of the room as fast as her legs would take her. "What she'd heard had frightened her badly, poor lady,"

John says. "It was obvious just by the way she talked about it. When I spoke with her, it was almost three months later, and she'd only just started going back to the study."

In the time between Mr. Bigby's first moan and John's investigation, the goings-on in the Cleveland home had gotten worse. "The lady seemed really nice," John says, "but the main reason I took the investigation was because I was practically guaranteed to experience a phenomenon of one sort or another. As of our last conversation before I flew to Ohio, she told me she was experiencing things at least three times a week. She'd agreed to have me over for a week-long investigation."

He arrived in Cleveland hauling two suitcases bursting with all sort of electronic recording devices and reference books. His hopes were high. "I was on a bit of a dry streak," John says. "But there was something about this one. My conversations with this lady had me convinced. I was sure that I was going to get some solid findings." That was one way to put it.

"I rigged the whole place up," the ghost hunter says. "I had two video recorders on tripods on both sides of the hall and two more in her study, with two audio recorders positioned around the corner where she told me the apparition materialized. At the time, I didn't own any EMF meters, but the entire time I was in the house, I was never more than arm's length away from my camera, my tape recorder and my infrared thermometer."

John arrived on a Thursday and planned to conduct his investigation until the following Wednesday. They quickly settled into a routine. After studying the audio and video recordings from the night before, John would step out with his lively client, spending most of the day outdoors, taking in the city. At night, John would power up all his equipment and begin his session.

"There was nothing too fancy about the nightly sessions," John says. "It was actually more like surveillance than active investigation. For the first two or three hours, I just made hourly rounds of the equipment, keeping my eyes and ears open for anything out of the ordinary. That would go on until 8:00 AM, when my host would go into her study and read for exactly two hours. It was like this every night; she lived by an incredibly set schedule."

For the first three nights, John spent those two hours in the study along with her. For two of those nights, he was vigilant the entire time, snapping photographs and taking temperature readings at the slightest sound. "She didn't seem to mind," John says. "I actually think she appreciated the company." The spirit didn't seem to, however. Thursday and Friday passed without a peep, and by Saturday night, John opened up a book of his own to help pass the time.

"By Sunday, I knew I'd have to change things up a bit," John says. Reasoning that the ghost had always shown a preference to the woman, and in all the years the family lived there, had never appeared to anyone else, John decided to spend Sunday night in another room. I was trying to keep my presence down to a minimum," he says. "The study hardly looked the same, with all my equipment, and I insisted she keep the study door open, but at least I wasn't there," he says. John headed to the living room while the woman went up to her study to get in her two hours of reading. John's hopes were high.

That night, at about 8:30 PM, footsteps sounded from the second floor. John shot up from the couch on the main floor. "There was a second where I wasn't sure if I heard it. The footsteps weren't coming from the study. She was still in the room. And the footsteps weren't booming. From where I was, it was a slow, careful walk; the creaking in the floorboards were almost louder than the footfalls."

But that would change. And fast. John describes the footsteps as getting louder with every step, until in a short matter of seconds they were heavy and fast, boldly stomping down the hall toward the woman's bedroom. Though John had come to believe the woman's accounts, he found himself having difficulty believing his own ears while it was occurring.

"I'm pretty sure there was a second or two where I froze," John confesses. "The footsteps were loud—far louder than I thought they would be. Something about it was really kind of eerie. And I'm still amazed how this lady had put up with this for the last several months."

John didn't waste too much time. He dashed up the stairs, tape recorder on, camera in his hands. "My understanding was that the footsteps never went along with an apparition. She'd never seen a man walking down the hall. She did say, though, that the second floor would always get chilly whenever she heard them. It wasn't chilly when I got to the top stairs. It was freezing. I'd experienced cold spots in the past, but never like that. It was so cold I felt as if I should have been able to see my breath." Taking a quick temperature measurement, John noted the reading: 44 °F.

It was cold, but there was nothing visible in the hallway. Nevertheless, John began snapping photos of the hall the moment he got there. This procedure is common among ghost hunters, who generally acknowledge that cameras occasionally capture images invisible or unnoticed by the naked eye. There was no one in the hallway, but John walked slowly, following the direction of the now-silent footsteps, taking pictures roughly every yard or so. When he got to the study, the door creaked open; the old lady's face peaked around the doorframe. "She asked with this sarcastic look if I had heard it, and I laughed," John says.

The woman laughed back, and when she did, the cold lifted. "It happened so quickly. This was really a dramatic temperature variation. It really was amazing," John says. The memory brought a trace of awe into his voice. "I asked her if it was always like this, with the cold, and she laughed again and said something like, 'Welcome to my home.'"

The rest of the night passed without event, and first thing next morning John woke eagerly, having potential findings to go over for the first time since he arrived. After making a quick trip to get the film he'd shot of the hallway developed, he headed back to the house to study the footage from the video cameras in the hallway and the audio recording from his tape recorder.

"The hard evidence I obtained that night was something of a disappointment," John says. "It's a recurring problem in these investigations, often the most impressive phenomena doesn't translate well onto the media when we try to capture it." At a first glance, the video cameras on either end of the hallway registered no activity until John himself appeared at the top of the stairs. Of course,

John played the tapes over and over, studying each replay closely. Was there no visible moving shape that coincided with footsteps? On some playbacks, he swore he could see a black blur moving across the dim hall, then he'd watch the footage again and decided that it was nothing but poor video quality and an overactive imagination. "One of the dangers paranormal investigators face is when they want so badly for a ghost to be there that they allow themselves to see ghosts in photographs, on video or on tape, when there's nothing actually there. It happens all the time. Half the ghost hunters out there are posting pictures of dust particles glowing off the camera flash and calling them orbs, or pictures of cigarette smoke in cemeteries become mysterious mists. It's quite sad."

John Davies is quick to state that his photographs turned up similarly poor results. "The audio recordings were a lot better, though," John says. On all four cameras in the hallway, you can distinctly hear the footfalls. The audio on the two by the bedroom door are really clear. The footsteps were moving towards these cameras, and they were getting louder as they were getting closer. Before they stop, they're practically booming on tape. As for the tape recorder I had on me," John continues, "I turned it on the moment I realized what was going on. You can hear the footsteps on that recorder, too, but not as clearly."

Modest evidence, perhaps, but it was only Monday. There were still three nights to go. That night, he recharged the batteries on all his equipment and covered the cameras in the hall and study with black drapes he'd bought earlier that day. Like the previous four nights,

John went about every hour to ensure the cameras in the hall were still there and functioning, and he did the same with the cameras and the tape recorders in the study. Eight o'clock came with everything prepared, and John went down to the living room while his host ensconced herself in her study.

The next two hours crawled by. Nothing was happening. More than once, John was tempted to go upstairs and look around but, adamant on sticking to the plan, he sat tight, intent on keeping a low profile. It was only when the clock struck 10 and he heard the study door open that John went up to speak with the old lady.

"I asked her if anything had happened to her, if he'd appeared and kept quiet—anything. She shook her head and made some remark about how he'd been uncharacteristically absent since I'd arrived." The evening proved to be uneventful, but when John walked in to shut off his equipment, his eyes fell on the heavily monitored corner. The two cameras he'd turned on two hours ago were still there, but there was only one tape recorder; the other was missing.

"She was completely unsurprised when I announced it," John says. "Things had been vanishing in her house for as long as she lived there. Barring her taking or hiding the recorder, we had another authentic paranormal incident on our hands." He went as far as to search her and the room, but the recorder was nowhere to be found.

"In all my years as an investigator," John says, "in all of my investigations, probably the one thing I regret most is that I didn't think to have another video camera trained on those tape recorders." He emits a low groan at the thought. "Anyway, I never got that recorder back."

Not only was he short a recorder, but the video footage of the study revealed nothing. Convinced by now that the house was indeed haunted, John still didn't have any tangible proof besides the sounds of footsteps on tape. From the onset, he had his heart set on the apparition. He wanted visual confirmation of the specter.

Hoping to make the investigation less obvious, John pulled the cameras in the study back from the walls, so the corner wouldn't be so crowded. This time he made sure the tape recorder was visible in one of the cameras, just in case the spirit got any ideas. All the cameras had their batteries fully charged and were concealed under drapes, ready to go. The next night, John waited.

It was some time past 9:00 PM when John heard the muffled exclamation from the second floor. His heart leapt. It was the old woman, and he swore he heard her faintly audible voice say something like "Oh! Hello!" Rising gingerly to his feet, he slowly crept up the stairs, lest the sound of his approach scare the spirit away. His own tape recorder was running; his camera was in his hands.

He was near the top of the stairs when the moaning began. "The sound that came out of that study was one of the eeriest things I've ever heard," John says. "I don't know if I can describe it, and I'm sure not going to imitate it."

He only stopped for a second, then redoubled his pace to the study. "Outside the door, the sound was loud. It was a deep, chalky, inhuman sound that went on and on and made my skin crawl. I was a bit worried about the woman. I don't know how she was able to take it. It was a terrible sound." John isn't sure how long he waited by the door. It could have been minutes, it could have been seconds, but the thing in the room was still groaning when he made up his mind to go in.

"I threw the door open with one hand and my camera in the other," John says. "I remember snapping a shot of the corner before I even looked." When he did look, however, it hit him that he'd been too late. "When I opened the door, there was no one in the room except the lady. She was sitting there staring at the corner of the room, and she didn't look happy. I can only imagine what it must have been like to be in the same room with that thing."

Unsure whether or not he'd taken the picture in time, John consoled himself that there was two video cameras set up in the corner. "I was sure that I had him!" he says.

That certainty quickly faded, however, as John strode over to the cameras. The power lights on his cameras were off. Picking the tape recorder, he saw that that too was dead. Then he noticed that the camera in his hands wasn't working either, and neither was the audio recorder he'd turn on when the moaning began. Everything had been working fine earlier. "For batteries to drain on recording equipment in the presence of ghosts is common. You read about it a lot in ghost hunters' reports, but I'd never seen it happen to so much equipment. Every recorder that was on that night had fully charged batteries!"

That would be the high point of John's Cleveland investigation. "After that, I had to admit that I was in over my head with this one," the ghost hunter says. "The next day, I started packing, and that night I only set up half my cameras. Nothing happened."

Today John has mixed feelings about the investigation. He still deeply regrets being unable to get any visual evidence of the phantom culprit.

"I spend a lot of time pursuing paranormal phenomena, and to have been able to witness something like that was a great thing. Then again, the only thing I walked away with were audio recordings of footsteps on tape. I couldn't help feeling let down."

After leaving Cleveland, he continued to correspond with the elderly woman. "My stay didn't have any effect on the spirit after all. That summer, it sounded like he was appearing more than ever. She called me once to tell me that my tape recorder turned up in the bathroom sink. In the fall, I starting to think that maybe I'd given up too easily, and wondered about going back for another try."

He never got the chance. The last John heard from the woman in the house was an e-mail he received in early October. "I assumed the worst and still haven't heard anything to this day, so I'm guessing I was right," John says. "She was up in years, and it seemed as if she'd lived a full life, but still, I was surprised at how her passing had gotten to me. Over the few months I'd known her, she'd become a friend. She still had so much wit and energy. It was sad to think she was gone."

And what of the ghost? Does the spirit of the mysterious old man still haunt the Cleveland home? Are there new inhabitants now coping with disembodied footsteps, sudden cold spots and missing personal possessions? Does the apparition of the silver-haired man still appear in the corner? Or was the ghost somehow connected to the old lady?

John Davies can't say for certain. He'd researched the history of the home before and after the investigation, both times turning up nothing. Despite his secret devotion to paranormal research, he hasn't contacted the new homeowners. "I decided some time ago to leave that house alone. In my mind, that ghost was somehow connected with the lady who lived there. This might not make any sense, but the big reason I won't go back is out of respect for her."

On the Coast

"Okay, I'll admit, California and ghosts don't exactly go together," says our next anonymous ghost hunter, who we'll call "Andrew Walsh" for the purposes of this story. "It's a beautiful state with all the sunshine, beaches, mountains, desert, trees. Probably in most people's minds, California is kind of about sunshine and the outdoors; ghosts are for the gloomy places."

Yet at the same time, Andrew concedes that there are ghosts even in the sunniest of places. "I wouldn't be spending so much of my time hunting them down if I hadn't seen any. But when I saw my first ghost, years and years ago, you could say that everything changed for me. I'm on a mission."

"Probably the less I say about my first paranormal experience the better," the young West Coast ghost hunter says, "it's a personal story, and not the sort of thing I'd want in a book about ghost stories. I can talk about the ghost that I saw south of Fort Bragg, just off the West Coast Highway, though."

Andrew begins, "I don't like to tell too many of my friends that I spend some of my spare time trying to find ghosts. With the razzing and all, I'm not too thrilled that about half the people I know think I'm nuts." Nevertheless, there are a few people, close friends, that Andrew has told, and it was one of these friends who told Andrew what happened on one of the beaches south of Fort Bragg in the summer of 2003.

"There was a group of tourists who'd come into town early in the morning. They stopped at a gas station to fill up, and my friend's friend was on the early shift that morning. These people were going on about what they'd seen on the beach the night before," Andrew says. "They asked my friend's friend if anyone knew about the *guy on the beach*."

According to the account Andrew received from his friend at the gas station, one of the campers had to go to the washroom the night before, and zipped out of the tent to find someplace to go. He'd just left the tent when he saw a man. The night was dark with only a sliver of moon in the sky, but the man appeared clearly against the black, crashing waters. He was visible because he was glowing slightly bluish white, as he walked along in the darkness. Now the sight of this glowing man must have instantly struck the camper as peculiar because he immediately ran over to his tent and shook his friends awake.

"My friend told me that they all saw him," Andrew continues. "He was walking along the shoreline, and he didn't even look at them as he moved past their tent. He was an old man, kind of glowing, and they could see through him. When he was about 20 yards or so away he vanished." As for the tourists, according to the gas jockey, they instantly packed up and relocated in their Jeep, where they spent the rest of the night talking about what they'd just seen.

"For sure I had to take the drive down to the beach," Andrew says. "I haven't had a chance to look into every ghost story I've ever heard, but it was summer holidays, and there wasn't anything else to do. So I packed, and right after work that Saturday, I drove down to the beach where they saw this man."

As casual as Andrew sounds when he talks about paranormal investigation, his actual methods are similar to
those of more experienced ghost hunters. He had packed
with him a tape recorder, a digital camera and infrared
thermometer. After arriving at the beach late in the afternoon, Andrew set up his tent, had something to eat and
waited. That night, he waited for several hours until he fell
asleep early in the morning. Andrew's first investigation
passed without a sighting, and he awoke to the sound of
the ocean's crashing waves late the next morning. But he
was nowhere near giving up.

"It's a good thing it was summer and I had the time on
my hands," he says. "I went back that night and two other
times that week. Each time, I didn't see a thing." Still,
Andrew wasn't discouraged and made plans to return the
following Sunday. "I know what people are going to
think," the young ghost hunter says. "Doesn't this guy
have a life? Going back over and over to this place because
people I don't even know said they saw a ghost?" The
question certainly crossed the author's mind.

"It might sound strange, but every night I went back to
that spot, I got the feeling the people had actually seen
this glowing man. I don't know how to explain it. There
was something about the beach at night. It was in the air,
or something. I was sure of it. I wasn't alone; something
was watching me. This place was haunted. I just had to
wait for the right time." It didn't help matters that Andrew
didn't own a video camera, and any attempt to set up an
audio recorder would be a waste of time against the sound
of the tides. All the ghost hunter could do was fight off

Andrew tried to photograph the specter, but all he captured on film was the beautiful coastal scenery.

sleep for as long as he was able and hope the ghost would eventually appear.

That Sunday, after so many vigilant nights, the long-awaited "right time" finally arrived. "At first, I wasn't sure whether to believe my eyes," Andrew says. "He showed up some time around 2:00 AM. I'd been reading a book by my flashlight when I saw something silver moving out of the corner of my eye. I looked up and it was him, about 30 yards away, walking along the water toward where I was."

Andrew picked up his camera with trembling hands. "As much as I was into ghost hunting, I'd never once taken a photograph of a ghost. Sure, I caught the occasional orb here and there, but personally, I don't much believe that orbs are anything more than dust on the camera lens. This was different. This was a full apparition, and he was coming right towards me. This guy on camera would be one of the greatest pictures of a ghost, ever."

Aware, however, that the apparition was still too far away to capture in the darkness, Andrew stepped out of his tent and walked toward the water slowly. "It was awesome. I could clearly make him out when he was about 20 yards away. He was old, and he was glowing silvery white, kind of like the moon. His eyes looked really heavy, and he was looking straight ahead. He didn't look too happy at all."

As Andrew grew closer, his own mood began to change. "I don't know if I can explain it," he says. "But it was getting stronger and stronger with every step I took towards him. There was this…heaviness…with this spirit that I can only call sad…and it was spreading to me. When I was about 10 yards away, I just wanted to lie down in the sand and get my bearings. It felt as though some-thing else was taking over my thoughts, and I needed to straighten myself out. I almost forgot that I had a camera in my hands and I was there to take pictures of this guy."

He almost forgot. But when the ghost was practically right in front of him, he was seized by wonder once again and realizing what he was there for, raised the camera and started snapping pictures. "I don't know how many I took," Andrew says. "I started shooting when he was profiled against the ocean, and kept going as he walked away from me. These were all great shots. He was showing up clear on my digital screen. I must have taken over 30 pictures."

Andrew kept snapping shots of the apparition until it vanished. "It's strange to think about now. My first real evidence of a ghost on camera, I should have been crazy excited, but as soon as he disappeared, the only thing I felt was tired…no…not just tired. I was exhausted. I felt as if I could have fallen asleep right there, standing up." Without even looking at the photos he'd taken, Andrew stumbled to his tent and fell asleep.

"There was quite a shock waiting for me the next morning," he says. "The old man was the first thing I thought of when I woke up, and I immediately grabbed my camera to take a look at the pictures. I think that morning had to be one of the most disappointing times of my life." There was nothing in his photos. He'd ended up taking well over 30 photographs, and there was nothing there but blackness and the occasional white cap on the ocean. Not even an orb.

Had he dreamt the whole thing? But there were the photos. Could he have been sleepwalking, then? Maybe getting up and walking through an incredibly vivid dream? He couldn't believe it. "I never really let that experience go," Andrew says, "and I can't really say that I figured it out, either. I put in a lot of research time afterward, but nothing came up on the beach. As far as the papers went, there was nothing about an old man; there were no murders or accidental deaths there."

Nevertheless, today Andrew refuses to believe that he might have imagined the old man. He says that he's enlarged one of the photos of the ocean at night, and it is framed and hanging on his wall. "He isn't visible there on camera," Andrew says, "but I know he's there. I'll make sure that I prove it, one way or another, the next time I go out." But for now, at least, the photos are black compositions, and Andrew will have to use his imagination.

4
Mission
Accomplished

Ghost Hunting for the People

For as far back as he can remember, Brad Mikulka has been fascinated with the paranormal. He didn't witness any ghostly apparitions drifting through his childhood years; he does not boast of a heightened sixth sense; there was never one defining moment in his life when he knew that he was destined to immerse himself in the spirit world. Brad's mother does claim that the family lived in a haunted house when he was two years old, but if the fledgling ghost hunter had any bizarre experiences at that age, they are buried deep in his memory, because he claims there was nothing especially extraordinary about his childhood.

There was just something about the idea of the dead existing alongside the living that always intrigued him. And it still intrigues him to this day. Brad's continued interest in the supernatural eventually led him to paranormal investigation. He joined the Southeast Michigan Ghost Hunting Society (SEMGHS) when it was founded in 1996, and eventually became the organization's second president. One of the original paranormal organizations in Michigan, the SEMGHS exists to provide a meeting ground for ghost devotees in Detroit and the surrounding area. It aims to educate individuals who have questions about the supernatural and also, perhaps above all, to assist people who have difficulties with spirits in their homes.

Mikulka long ago stopped feeling surprised by the number of hauntings in his area. "Ghosts are everywhere," the SEMGHS's president asserts. "Contrary to the general theory among investigators, there doesn't have to be

a traumatic history for there to be a ghost in the area."
The SEMGHS theory has two significant implications for
ghost hunters. First, Brad's belief in a world populated by
a ghostly citizenry—existing just beyond our senses—
downplays the traditional ghost hunter's practice of digging into a place's history to come up with an explanation
for a haunting. Second, such a belief demands a greater
vigilance from ghost hunters because it implies that there
are many more ghosts on the earth than is commonly
believed. With spirits potentially lurking behind every
corner, ghost hunters must always be ready for a supernatural encounter.

I'm not saying that they're never warned of the presence of ghosts beforehand. Indeed, Mikulka states that 90
percent of the SEMGHS's investigations are in private res-
idences, and the society is so busy that it is currently
booked for the next two months. He feels a certain responsibility when he takes a look at clients' homes. "When a
person contacts us, they usually need our help. They might
have a situation that they can't take anymore; they may
have just moved into an old house and are having all kinds
of trouble—whatever it is, we do everything we can to
educate them about what is going on. We analyze footage
of the investigation, we have psychics go over the place
with us, and we get back to the residents of the home as
quickly as we can, usually within 30 days. Often, these people aren't so much frightened of the ghosts themselves, but
they're just looking for some peace of mind—somebody
to tell them that they aren't going crazy."

While the SEMGHS president is often obliged to keep
the findings of these forays secret, investigations that take

place in the confines of people's homes almost always offer more intimate contact with spirits than do studies of the other ghost hunters' favorite investigating sites— wide-open cemeteries. According to Mikulka, this may be because haunted houses are usually tied to tragic mortal circumstances specific to those people who lived in the homes, whereas the largely nameless energies haunting cemeteries are bound only by the resting place of their remains. To be sure, many grave site ghosts do have well-documented histories, but for the most part, the ghosts that haunt houses are paranormal entities that are most closely linked with their human pasts—they have identifiable histories, purposes or possessions that keep them here long after their bodies are gone.

Such was the case for a house in Troy that a SEMGHS team investigated late in the fall of 1998. A SEMGHS investigator named Nick Sikes called Brad about strange things that were happening in the place he was renting.

Nick had taken up the habit of carrying a camera around with him at home after catching fleeting movements out of the corner of his eyes several times. It usually happened when he was lying on the couch, just as his mind was wobbling over that line that separates sleep from consciousness. Moments before his head dropped, Nick would catch dark shadows moving quickly across the hall, causing him to suddenly awake and bolt to his feet.

The breaking point came one night when he was woken by a strong, almost suffocating scent. Roses. It was as if a mountain of the flowers loomed just beyond his sight in the darkness of his room. That, or somebody had sprayed a dozen cans of rose air-freshener into the room and closed the door. Jumping quickly out of his bed, Nick yelled to whatever was in his room to get out while simultaneously snapping a photo in the darkness. Later, when he got a chance to look at the picture he had taken, he saw two orbs hovering in the blackness of the photograph. Brad organized an investigation of Nick's house as soon as he laid eyes on the photo of the two celluloid orbs that Nick sent to him.

Of all the investigations the SEMGHS conducted in the house, the visit in late August 2001 that stands out for Brad. That night, five other SEMGHS members accompanied Brad: his wife, Brenda, two psychics and two supernatural mediums. The SEMGHS president doesn't have a heightened sense with the supernatural, so he usually has at least two more psychically gifted members present during SEMGHS investigations. According to Brad, psychics are able to see spiritual entities more readily than most of us, while mediums are gifted in their ability to actually communicate with these ghostly beings. The entire team would witness amazing supernatural activity on this investigation.

Not only did Brad and Brenda capture some impressive photographs at Nick's house, but the psychics and mediums were kept busy as well. For reasons that were about to be partially explained, at least two ghosts dwelled in the Troy household. Things got weird when the Mikulkas' digital photos registered bright white areas on the photo frames that were taken in complete darkness. These photographs weren't the typical orbs; Brad wasn't sure what they were dealing with. "We had no idea how those white blurs got there. It was like somebody was standing too close to the camera when the flash went off."

In one room where the psychics sensed a lot of activity, Brenda took a picture of the darkness, capturing the faint image of a human neck, shoulder and arm on her digital camera. But it was not until the team wandered outside the house that the investigation took a sharp turn in the direction of the bizarre.

"Our psychics sensed a lot of activity just behind the house, when one of our mediums picked up a name: Conan. Apparently, he was a farmer from the early 1900s, and the land we were standing on used to be his farm plot." No sooner had the paranormal team gleaned this information when one of the psychics suddenly felt a sharp pain move up her left arm and into her chest. The woman was then suddenly aware that the farmer had suffered a heart attack in his last moments of life; the pain in her arm and chest was the last thing the farmer felt before he died. He was resting against a tree that still stood in the backyard when a number of snakes darted up at him and bit his arm. It wasn't poison, but fear that killed him. Severely startled by the striking serpents, Conan's heart stopped and he died right there under the tree.

Brenda took a picture of the tree in the yard, and sure enough, there in the digital display of her camera was the partial apparition of a man, just like the shot of the neck, arm and shoulder taken inside the house. It became clear that Conan, who was still sitting by the tree, was a soul completely lost. Indeed, almost a century after he died, he was still unable to come to terms with his sudden and meaningless death. The SEMGHS was determined to help.

One of the mediums in the yard stepped in. "Do you see a light?" the woman asked Conan. "There are people who you know and love who will come and get you and take you into the light." The farmer responded to the medium that there were indeed eight "lights" hovering near him. At that moment, Brenda took a picture of the tree, and there in the photograph were eight orbs of light floating next to a white mist. The SEMGHS medium then helped Conan pass over to the other side. "Go with them into the light; you'll be at peace," she said. Brad snapped about five pictures a few moments later and saw nothing there but the old tree in the night. It seems that Conrad's soul finally did cross over to where it belonged.

Another spirit resided with Nick but didn't seem to be in such a rush to get to the afterlife. In fact, Nick could only stare in shock when one of the mediums called out his grandfather's name while communicating with one of the house's ghosts. It seems that Nick's grandfather was still protective of his grandson; his spirit kept close watch over him. Suddenly Nick's recurring feeling that he was not alone even when nobody else was in the room—as well as the light blurs and discolorations that hovered over him in numerous photographs through much of his life—made sense. While Conan could only find peace when he joined the other spirits, Nick's grandfather did not want to leave the land of the living. Thus the SEMGHS investigation in the Troy house was concluded…guiding one lost soul into the light and reuniting a man with the spirit of his grandfather.

ORION and the Haunted Machine Shop

It's difficult to think of a better way to express the science–spiritualism divide of paranormal investigation than Michael Sinclair's opening statement on his ghost-hunting group's web site:

> ORION is composed of a team of dedicated, highly trained paraprofessionals whose investigative intelligence-gathering techniques and superior analyzing skills produce conclusive scientific validation of the phenomena you are experiencing.

ORION, which stands for Otherside Research & Investigations of New England, uses scientific methods that group founder Michael Sinclair goes on to explain:

> After analyzing the data from our preliminary mission we will make another appointment with the owner to return for a further in-depth investigation and attempt at counseling the entity to cross over.

Michael says that while his organization is generally successful at persuading spirits to cross over, some spirits resist their attempts and persist on haunting the sites they're drawn to.

This approach to paranormal investigation actually makes ORION a bit of an anomaly among other ghost hunters. While most paranormal groups limit their activities to observation and documentation of supernatural phenomena, ORION actively attempts to engage ghosts, hoping to aid them in "crossing over."

The basic idea here is that many ghosts are tortured spirits, unwilling or unable to let go of their earthly lives. Some ghosts aren't even aware they're dead, while others—obsessed with the circumstances of their deaths, or refusing to abandon the things they loved while they were living—linger out of fear, love, hate or sheer stubbornness. According to this theory, most ghosts are essentially victims—entities that are stuck, trapped in endless cycles of negative emotion. ORION aims to help liberate them from these cycles.

What does it mean to cross over? Basically, anyone who's seen the movie *Ghost* has a general idea of what crossing over means. If ghosts are spirits that are bound to earth one way or another, crossing over is what they do when, for whatever reason, they finally cut their ties to the earth and take the step (cross over) to whatever is waiting for them on the other side. The religious implications of this philosophy are obvious, and ORION makes no excuses about its melding of scientific and spiritual methods. Sinclair is an advocate of stringent scientific methods when it comes to gathering evidence of ghosts, but the principal psychic in his group, Gary McKinstry, is an ordained minister.

Nowhere is ORION's divide between science and spirituality more evident than in its founder, Michael Sinclair himself. As an executive sitting on the board of a multinational corporation, Sinclair had an early interest in engineering that pushed him to pursue a bachelor degree with a double major in science and business. At the same time, an abiding interest in psychic phenomena pushed him towards the fringe sciences, where he pursued metaphysical studies in organizations such as the Rosicrucian Order and the Berkeley Psychic Institute. Ultimately, the confluence of science and the supernatural steered Sinclair into ghost hunting. He moved to Massachusetts in August 2002, and served as the chief investigator of another paranormal group before establishing ORION in February 2004. The following is one of ORION's first investigations.

"I was at my desk on a blustery evening when I received a call from my colleague, Gary McKinstry," Sinclair begins. "He received an interesting call from a machine shop owner who'd been having all sorts of things happening in his shop." Gary was ORION's number one psychic, and he didn't need to talk Michael into getting on board with the investigation.

"This man had told Gary that all sorts of weird phenomena had been occurring for a while," Michael says, "but being a skeptic at heart, he'd learned to disregard the footsteps and low laughter that he often heard in his shop when he was there alone." The shop owner wasn't the only one who'd heard the sounds. "Some of his family experienced the same kind of things," Michael continues. "The disembodied footsteps and laughter had become a conversation piece in the man's house. He told Gary that, more than once, the shop computers had switched on by themselves in the middle of the night." Even the family dog had suspicions things weren't quite right in the machine shop—as a rule he only entered the building when there was a tempting enough treat waiting inside, or when someone pulled hard on his leash.

The shop owner had managed to convince himself that all the events were the product of an overactive imagination. But one night, when he looked up from his computer monitor to see a full-length apparition of a man dressed in an archaic 19th-century suit and a stovepipe hat standing on the other side of the room, he decided it was time to take action. "Because," as Michael puts it, "the unknown paranormal force was now making the night shift even more agonizing than normal." The specter hadn't done anything harmful, but the shop owner wasn't thrilled about its presence, and he called Gary hoping his organization could do something about it.

Following ORION procedures, Michael contacted someone else associated with the purported haunting to test the validity of the shop owner's claim. In this case, it was the man's wife, and she corroborated everything her husband told Gary in the first phone call. Everything checked out, and a time was set for the first investigation.

"The evening we arrived was gray and overcast," Michael says. "I drove to the shop owner's home for a final round of questions, this time with the husband, to make sure the story Gary and I had heard was the same." It was and, satisfied that the shop owner was being honest, Michael had him sign a formal consent form allowing ORION to investigate.

Michael left for the investigation site with the shop owner's family, meeting up with Gary McKinstry and his wife Virginia when he got there. Michael and Gary were the first ORION members in the shop, and they took a short tour of the interior to familiarize themselves with the site before bringing their equipment in. "Almost immediately, Gary and I noticed the heaviness in the air," Michael says. Going purely on intuition, both men felt a presence at the shop, as if whatever was there was dying to know who they were and what they were doing.

When they left the building, ORION photographer and clairaudient Sharon had arrived. She took a quick tour of the building and got the same feeling as Michael and Gary. They were all convinced there was something in the shop. As it turned out, their findings would confirm their premonitions.

During their first foray into the shop, Michael's team measured cold spots, photographed some great images of ectoplasmic mist, videotaped footage of floating orbs and measured more than one spike in the local electromagnetic field with their EMF meters. All the while they were collecting this data, they were also trying to make contact with the spirit. "I'm convinced that at one point, the spirit passed right through me," Michael relates. "I was standing there when all of a sudden I felt a coolness and a momentary loss of equilibrium. Gary, who'd been standing about 10 feet away from me, asked 'Did you feel that?'"

Gary went through the shop slowly, asking questions out loud and hoping to channel the entity through him so they could communicate with it and perhaps learn what was keeping it from crossing over. He had limited success.

"The spirit would repeatedly make a connection with Gary and then break off," Michael remembers. It was therefore difficult to get detailed information about the spirit, but they were able to learn something of its motivations. "Gary got the general idea that there was nothing malevolent about this ghost," Michael continues, "but that it was intensely interested in the shop."

What was so interesting about the shop? "According to the spirit, 'what wasn't interesting about the shop?'" Michael says. "It was wondering about all the machines—what they did and why they were there." During one of Gary's longer connections with the ghost, they learned that the ghost was actually entertaining a slightly condescending attitude about the shop owner's hardware. "The ghost communicated that it didn't mean anyone any harm, but believed that 'all these new-fangled contraptions were mucking the handiwork of skilled craftsmen.'"

After a few rounds and only limited communication with the spirit, the trio headed outside for a short break. The shop owner and his family peppered the investigators with anxious questions when they emerged. Had they seen the ghost? Was it still there? Did they manage to get it to cross over?

Michael was quick to assure the family that they'd made contact with the spirit in the shop, and that it didn't mean any harm. He told them that it seemed to be more curious than anything else; it was intrigued by all the machines in the shop and hadn't meant to frighten them. As for getting the ghost to cross over, Michael told them that was precisely what they were about to try.

They wasted no time when they resumed the investigation. It was time for Michael Sinclair to attempt a conversation with the spirit. "I gathered the equipment and proceeded to go back inside and hook up the digital audio equipment," the ORION founder says. "Sharon, Gary and

I shut off all the lights and closed the doors, and gathered close to our recording equipment."

Michael then began asking questions of the darkness. "What is your name?"

Silence.

"Why are you here?"

No response.

"What do you want? Do you have a message for us?"

Still nothing.

And then Michael asked the big question. "Are you aware that you're dead?"

There was still no answer. A moment passed before Michael, unfazed by the silence, urged the spirit to cross over. "Step toward the light," he said. "This isn't the place for you anymore."

That was when the spirit finally responded. "I'd just finished speaking, and we were standing there in silence when we heard the sound of footsteps shuffling in the far corner," Michael says. "Then, out of that same corner, came (the sound of) low, very distinct laughter." Michael looked at his colleagues to see if they were hearing the drawn-out chuckling. Both Gary and Sharon nodded; they heard it too.

Michael turned to face the laughter. "What's so funny?" he asked aloud.

The laughter stopped, and there was silence for several moments before it started up again.

"At least he's got a sense of humor," Gary said.

Unfortunately, the three ghost hunters weren't let in on what made the dead laugh. Despite the investigators' questioning, they received no response. "I repeated some of my previous questions in hopes of capturing more on the recorder," Michael says. But these questions were greeted with more silence.

Gary McKinstry spoke up at that point. The psychic minister stepped toward the one corner and began addressing the spirit, urging it to move on, to cross over and leave the shop owner and his family in peace. It was impossible to know what the spirit thought of the minister's suggestion. Had Gary gotten through to it? Had the ghost decided to abandon its fascination with the machines in the building and move on? It was impossible to tell.

Sharon, Gary and Michael stood still and silent for a few more long moments, listening intently for any sounds. And then, just when it seemed like it might be a closed case, the shuffling in the corner resumed, followed by the sound of a corrugated iron box being dragged across the concrete floor. The ghost was still there.

By this point, ORION had been on site for nearly three hours. It was getting late, and it was time to call it a night. Though their attempts at getting the ghost to cross over weren't quite successful, at least they'd acquired substantial information on the haunting, and could always come back to try again.

Michael announced that the investigation was over, crossed the room and switched on the lights. They began packing up. "Sharon was taking down the video camera and I was unhooking the audio equipment while Gary began blessing the shop, as he did after every investigation.

"I was wrapping up the audio when a huge noise sounded from the inside of the front office area," Michael says. "It was a loud slam, as if a door was being slammed shut. The noise was so loud it was audible to the owner and his family outside. Later they told us that they thought we might have dropped one of the huge metal tools in the shop on the floor."

Of course, the ghost hunters hadn't dropped anything, and what's more, no door in the shop had been slammed shut. Like a modest little thunderclap, the booming sound had come out of nowhere. Unlike thunder, however, there was no ready explanation—until, that is, ORION's follow up.

"Our second visit to the shop revealed a different scene all together," Michael says. "We recorded significantly diminished EMF readings, there was nothing in our photos and we detected little to no psychic energy." Furthermore, the shop owner told them he hadn't experienced anything out of the ordinary after their first visit.

It seems that the ghost in the machine shop heeded Gary's advice in the end, and it crossed over, just as the minister suggested. "We have a theory that the spirit decided to cross over after Gary had blessed the shop," Michael says. Presumably, the ghost was responsible for the banging noise that sounded the instant Gary concluded his blessing. Though ghosts don't commonly make a commotion when crossing over, this spirit apparently chose to make its exit with a bang.

As for the origin of the haunting, Michael can't say for certain where the ghost came from. "While the structure itself was built fairly recently, there's no accounting for the land it was built on," the expert ghost hunter says. "We believe there was psychic energy stored within the building site. The ghost that chose to make this place its haunt was, as we discovered, not a hostile presence, but was there out of curiosity."

Mere curiosity might seem a strange reason for a spirit to haunt a place. Perhaps it makes more sense when we consider what the ghost was curious about—the machines in the shop—that is to say, technology. Think about how curious our plasma screen televisions, computers and DVDs would seem to people who passed on only 10 years ago, never mind how our current industrial technology would appear in the eyes of a man from the 19th century.

Curiosity indeed. How many of us living today would choose to haunt a Sony Store or Apple Computers dealership 100 years from now, just to get a peek at the hardware of the next century? Probably more of us than we'd like to think.

Demons in Connecticut

It's commonly said that the practice of paranormal investigation is where science and the supernatural intersect. The best ghost-hunting groups are those that are able to combine strict empirical methods with the subjective—and most unscientific—intuiting of psychic premonition. Yet there's another aspect of paranormal investigation, one that's often ignored by most mainstream ghost hunters: religion.

A number of obvious reasons exist as to why most ghost hunters choose to steer clear of religion. For one, a group's religious affiliation potentially alienates people who don't identify with that belief system. Second, the nature of paranormal investigation entails active questioning of the afterlife while most religions tells us to accept the afterlife on faith, so the practice of ghost hunting is often outside the fold of most organized religions.

But not always. Some ghost hunters out there include formal religion in their methods. In fact, some ghost hunters feel as though they have no choice but to do so. These investigators are the ones whose experiences with the supernatural have convinced them that religion can be a very real, very powerful force.

John Zaffis is one such investigator. With over 30 years of paranormal study under his belt, Zaffis is definitely among the more seasoned investigators operating today. And if his three decades pursuing paranormal phenomena have taught him anything, it's that there are definite lines of good and evil in the world of spirits. On more than one occasion, his investigations have led him over to the wrong side of that line.

Zaffis' experiences with the supernatural have taken him on a different trajectory from most other paranormal investigators. While standard ghost-hunting activities tend to be limited to observation, documentation and basic communication with purported spirits, Zaffis has anchored his paranormal oeuvre in deeper waters. For Zaffis, supernatural mysticism has always come with a heavy religious strain. From almost the onset of his ghost-hunting career, Zaffis has been set in this direction.

It began with an early affiliation with the two investigators in his family: his uncle Ed Warren and Ed's wife, Lorraine. The Warrens, who published two books about their own investigations, *Graveyards* and *In A Dark Place*, had a lasting influence on Zaffis. He began studying demonology under their guidance, and soon after was participating in cases that featured possession and exorcism.

Zaffis worked with some of the premier authorities, from Roman Catholic priests and rabbis and Buddhists to different Christian ministers in these matters. As well as traveling all across the United States and Canada, Zaffis has also taken his research into parts of the United Kingdom. In the 30 years he's been at it, Zaffis has investigated several thousand cases, and he is considered one of the more respected members of the paranormal community today.

It hasn't been an easy road. Anyone seen *The Exorcist*? People usually have to be pushed pretty far to call for an exorcism. Whether it is an individual or a home that is afflicted by the most virulent kind of haunting, exorcism is never easy to deal with.

Zaffis learned first-hand just how difficult an exorcism can be back in the summer of 1988, when Ed and Lorraine Warren were called in to take a look at the goings-on in a Connecticut home. To this day, almost 20 years later, the nine-week investigation stands out as one of Zaffis' most difficult experiences with the supernatural. It was nine weeks of the worst kind of paranormal activity a person could witness, culminating in an encounter that John Zaffis would never be able to forget. And it all began with a phone call.

Carmen Snedeker called Ed and Lorraine Warren in late August. Right away, it was obvious to the Warrens that something was very wrong. Carmen and her husband Al had moved from their upstate New York home to Connecticut to be closer to the hospital where their son was being treated for Hodgkin's Disease. Carmen and Al were finding the regular commutes between New York and Connecticut more and more difficult. One day Carmen was driving around near the hospital when she spotted a 'For Rent' sign in front of a house that was being renovated. Stopping in to take a closer look, she saw that there were three bedrooms on the main floor, exactly what her family needed. Then and there, she decided to rent the place.

Who knows if Carmen would have made the same decision if she'd bothered to look downstairs. It wasn't until moving day two weeks later that her husband emerged from basement with a surprised look on his face. "Did you know this was an old funeral home?" Al asked.

Carmen returned her husband's look. "No! How do you know that?"

Al led her down the stairs. The renovators had taken care of the main floor but had left the basement practically untouched. It was full of the tools that undertakers use to do their work. Well, the Snedekers weren't too happy to discover that their new home was once used to house dead people and prepare them for burial or cremation. Still, they allowed natural optimism to prevail and continued with the unpacking, trying to put all thoughts of embalmed corpses out of their minds. They probably would have stopped packing and left the house immediately if they had known half of what was in store for them.

The troubles with the Snedekers' son began almost immediately after they settled into the new place. He was hearing voices incessantly and was terrified of being alone in his room at night. He saw the shadows in the darkness, right before a man in the black pin-stripe suit would appear at his bedside.

Voices? Shadows? A man in a pin-stripe suit? The concerned Snedekers took their son to the hospital, where he was shortly diagnosed with schizophrenia so acute that they recommended having him removed from the house. Believing they were doing what was best for their son, Al and Carmen did what the doctors recommended and had their son institutionalized.

It wasn't long, however, before they began to doubt the doctors' diagnosis. All sorts of strange and terrifying things began to happen to them. On more than one occasion, Carmen was attacked by invisible hands. Her cousin

Tammy was similarly harassed. Once, when Carmen was trying to help her cousin with whatever was assaulting her, the rosary she'd taken to carrying around shattered in her hands.

That was when Al and Carmen decided to call to the Warrens for help. John Zaffis was still working closely with his uncle and aunt, and he went along with them to look over the Connecticut home. As crazy as things would get during the investigation, it was John, and John alone, who witnessed the worst of it.

From almost the moment they arrived, Ed, Lorraine and John knew that they were not dealing with a mere haunting. No, diabolical forces were at work in this house. The shattered rosary wasn't the only indication. Unlike standard hauntings, which tend to exhibit recurring phenomena that are often predictable in their repetition, the occurrences in the Snedeker rental home were getting worse day by day. The personal attacks were escalating, the cold spots that would suddenly form in the house were getting colder, whatever was in the house was getting angrier and bolder. Everyone felt that if something wasn't done soon, the situation could spiral out of control.

They decided to get the clergy involved, and priests came in and blessed the home. Things calmed instantly. Three days passed in complete peace. It didn't even feel like the same house, as if the things that had previously occurred had been a bad dream. But after the third day, the nightmare came back—with a vengeance.

Now, the entire family—Carmen, Al and Tammy—was experiencing attacks at the same time and, the attacks lasted longer. The only warning of the attacks was a sudden cold that descended over the house, and each time the cold got colder. They called the clergy in again, and once more the priests blessed the house. Three days passed without incident, and then, just as before, the terror resumed. And it continued to get worse every day.

Things got so bad that no one dared to venture anywhere in the house alone. The invisible hands that attacked residents and investigators alike seemed to grow stronger with every onslaught. Near the end, the environment was so hostile that Zaffis and the Warrens didn't feel that it was safe to leave the Snedekers in the house by themselves, and the three investigators took to camping in the living room at night. Every night, they were kept awake by the sound of fluttering along the floor and walls; it grew louder with each evening. Near the end, the fluttering got so pronounced that they could feel it—they could feel the invisible appendages of the malevolent creatures that darted around them.

As tough as it was for everyone involved, John Zaffis alone experienced the peak of the Snedeker house possession. "I was sitting at the dining room table when it started to get ice cold in the room. At this point, I knew something was getting ready to happen," Zaffis explains. He called out to everyone in the house, but received no response. Everyone was usually on the alert, but where was everyone?

Zaffis had a foreboding realization. The other people in the house couldn't hear him because this cold didn't affect them. The cold had come only for him—something in the house was waiting for him. "I knew at this point that this was meant for me to experience alone," Zaffis

John watched in horror as the demon descended the staircase.

says. "I'd gotten up and walked into the hallway and looked up at the top of the stairs." The smell hit him immediately. "I began to smell something like rotting meat," he remembers. "It was unbearable."

And then *it* appeared. "As I continued to look up the grand staircase, I started to see something begin to form as it slowly descended the staircase. A murky mass of rippling green, the figure was vaguely human, standing over six feet tall, with two dark red circles in the place where eyes might have been. It was the ugliest thing I'd ever seen, and it had come to the last step on the staircase."

Then this thing stopped and spoke to John: "Do you know what it did to us? Do you know?"

"That was enough for me," John states. "I left the home and didn't return for three days. I don't think I've ever encountered anything that has scared me as bad as that." Indeed, the encounter terrified John so badly that he wasn't able to speak for days. But his voice returned along with his sense of responsibility. He couldn't forget his duties and knew the Snedekers and his fellow investigators needed his help. After three days' rest, he returned to help the family. John had no doubts that the house was possessed; the thing on the stairs was, to borrow his words, "a full-formed demon." And not just any full-formed demon, but the first one that he'd ever seen with his own eyes. "It's something that until my dying day, I'll never forget."

The encounter on the stairs was the last straw. It was time to bring out the big guns. If demons were what the Snedekers had on their hands, then Al, Lorraine and John would recommend the most drastic anti-demon measure available: exorcism.

When the day came, three priests arrived at the Connecticut home to perform the rites of exorcism. According to John, the air in the house was charged. There was a sense that something big was going to happen. Having endured the demons in the house for nine weeks, the Snedeker family and the investigators just knew that whole affair wouldn't be concluded peacefully. They wouldn't be disappointed.

As soon as the three priests began the rite of exorcism, the entire house began to shake. "The dishes were rattling, the pictures on the wall were rattling and anything within the house was shaking and banging," John remembers. It grew more intense as the priests proceeded, reaching an apex just as they were concluding the ritual.

When the last words were uttered, the priests, the investigators and the Snedekers found themselves in a totally different house. "The smell of roses came upon us," John remembers, "and we all knew at that point that something divine was taking place and it was over." The house had been exorcised; the demons were gone.

Or that's what the priests claimed. Even if it were true, the Snedekers had already accumulated too many bad memories there, divinely cleansed or not. They moved out soon after that, and though their new home was just blocks from the former funeral home, they've never been bothered by any paranormal activities since. So whatever had attracted the malevolent forces to their former home, couldn't have been anything personal.

Which leaves us with the question of the house. What was it about the former funeral home that made it such a conduit for dark forces? Like so many other questions concerning the paranormal, we can only guess. Perhaps what transpired in the Connecticut house that summer would be best left in the past. Those readers so inclined will be happy to leave the story here. For those others whose natural dispositions compel them to examine the slimy things that live under every rock, the Warrens and the Snedekers wrote a book titled *In A Dark Place*, which features the events in the possessed household during the course of the Warren/Zaffis investigation.

The ABCs of
Ghost Hunting on MTV

If you're a ghost hunter and you live in North America, chances are you know about The Atlantic Paranormal Society (TAPS). Founded by ghost-hunting godfathers Jason Hawes and Grant Wilson, TAPS is a large paranormal umbrella organization that includes some of the most accomplished investigators on the continent on its list of affiliates and friends. More than one of the investigators featured in this book is associated with the TAPS nationwide network. From Patty Wilson in Pennsylvania to Richard Smith in Texas, TAPS is able to connect people with the best ghost hunters in their regions.

But Jason Hawes and Grant Wilson's organization isn't purely a network of investigators. Not at all. Based in the northeast United States, TAPS boasts a large, experienced base of investigators, researchers, interviewers, demonologists and administrators all working to study and explore paranormal phenomena, while aiding and educating those who've come in contact with forces they don't understand. TAPS is a prolific ghost-hunting group, whose numerous (and often sensational) explorations of haunted locales have made them well known, not only within the subculture of ghost hunters, but among the public as well.

Of course, the television spots don't hurt. Whatever it is about Jason and Grant, they've enjoyed (or, depending on your attitude, have been cursed with) an inordinate amount of media attention compared to so many of their peers. In fact, at the time of this writing, October 2004, their organization was being featured on the SciFi Channel in a weekly documentary series called—of all things—*Ghost Hunters*. The show follows the ghost hunters and their affiliates through their investigations. Though Jason and Grant were busy with their October commitments, TAPS historian and demonologist Keith Johnson was able to provide some information about the intrepid ghost-hunting duo's first major televised investigation—appropriate, considering TAPS' current national exposure on *Ghost Hunters*.

In 1999, MTV was developing a show called *FEAR*. For those who don't remember, *FEAR* was a paranormal reality show, for lack of a better description, where real-life ghost hunters were filmed going into a purportedly haunted site to determine whether or not it was actually haunted. In the course of its two-season stint, more than one paranormal expert was reduced to tears by what they experienced on camera.

The producers of the show had contacted Jason and Grant, asking them if they were interested in participating in an investigation of the long-abandoned Fairfield Hills State Hospital, in Fairfield, Connecticut. The hospital was renamed as the St. Agnes Mental Asylum on the show, perhaps because it sounds creepier, or perhaps to keep curiosity-seekers from flooding to the deserted compound.

Whatever the case, the name wasn't too important. The Fairfield Hills State Hospital was indeed a former mental asylum, composed of five deserted buildings that had an astonishing reputation for being haunted. It's easy to see why. Forget that the deserted buildings—with their peeling walls, empty hallways and rooms scattered with archaic medical equipment—just look spooky. Anyone who knows anything about the history of psychiatry might have an idea about the unpleasant things that once went on within those walls.

In America, the medical institution's approach to mental patients has improved dramatically over the years. Early asylums functioned primarily to keep the mentally insane apart from society, and little else. Almost no thought or care was put into the living conditions of these inmates, and asylums were squalid and inhuman places, where inmates suffered from untold deprivation and abuse, if not lifelong and crippling boredom.

Things only got worse when psychiatry started using electrotherapy in mental hospitals across the nation in the 1950s. Its questionable efficacy aside, this treatment was never popular among patients, and doubtless hundreds of inmates were dragged kicking and screaming to these agonizing sessions. There were darker tales about what went on in Fairfield Hills. As Keith Johnson states, "It was rumored that some of the inmates at St. Agnes were often literally used as human guinea pigs in such experimental therapies as electric shock treatment, psychotropic drugs and untried corrective surgeries."

Jason and Grant met MTV's production crew—Dave, the production manager and Matt, his assistant—for the first time outside of the old hospital on a fall afternoon in 1999. Presumably because the show was in its earliest stages of production (the sequences they would shoot on this day were actually aired as the second part of the pilot episode), Dave knew very little about the technicalities of hauntings and ghost hunting.

What would you expect to find in a place like this?" Dave asked them. As investigators, Jason and Grant hesitated at drawing conclusions or making assumptions about a site before taking a look. Jason told the MTV man that he nevertheless suspected there'd be a good chance of coming into contact with some residual activity, the type of haunting an investigator is most likely to come across. "The best way to describe it, I suppose, is like trapped energy. Technically, there isn't really even an entity present, only the energy," Jason explained.

Educating the countless frightened homeowners and supernatural eyewitnesses is part of being a ghost hunter, so Grant stepped in at this point and added, "A residual haunting is typically an event that is repeated over and over. It may happen every night or every week or even every year. Most often, the repeated event tends to be something specific. Perhaps it's some traumatic event which an individual or individuals experienced; perhaps it's even what was experienced at the moment of death."

This kind of phenomenon isn't considered sentient or aware, but more like an automatic psychic replay. Ghost hunters often use the analogy of a tape or video playing the same segment over repeatedly. Often it is the residue of a particularly powerful emotion that someone once felt. With residual energies, ghost hunters can do very little. The best they can do with these hauntings is inform people that there's nothing inherently harmful or malevolent about residuals. They're about as dangerous (and, okay, as annoying) as a train that regularly rumbles by a home.

But then there's the other basic kind of haunting, which is considered an intelligent haunt. "In this situation, the entity or entities are actually aware of their surroundings. Unlike a residual haunt, most of the time you'll find that in an intelligent haunt, the spirits aren't necessarily confined to one particular spot—they can move about freely. Also, they'll acknowledge the existence of human beings and may even attempt to communicate with them in certain ways," Jason explained.

More than anything else, these ghosts are trying to get people to notice them. Their motivations for haunting a place were significant to them while they were living. The classic example is the spirit in the haunted house— the person had become so attached to the home while it was alive that it refused to leave, even after death. Often, this ghost views subsequent residents as intruders and will become hostile. But not always.

"These spirits can be benevolent or mischievous, depending upon the reason they're haunting a location," Jason adds. Sometimes (as seen in the movie, *Sixth Sense*) these spirits don't even know they're dead. Often the ghosts want more than anything else to just be noticed by the living, and they tend to gravitate to people who are perceptive to their presence—such as psychics and children. If these spirits feel that no one can see them, they'll often take measures to get noticed. All the typical symptoms of the haunted house come from these activities to get noticed: the disembodied footsteps, the banging on the walls, the slamming doors, the flickering lights and the misplaced items. And sometimes, though very rarely, they appear as apparitions.

With the crash course in hauntings out of the way, Jason and Grant readied themselves for a preliminary walk through the site. Dave was skeptical, but since he was the man in charge of the camera work, he was going with Jason and Grant to get an idea of what they would be doing and the best way to capture their activities on camera. There was no electricity in the asylum, so his crew prepared to have their generators ready for the equipment for the shooting that night.

For the next couple of hours, Dave, Matt and a few others from the MTV crew tagged along with Jason and Grant around the asylum. With EMF meters ready and eyes peeled for anything unusual, they made a quick tour of the five empty structures, and Jason and Grant determined that two of the buildings showed the most potential for paranormal activity. Both buildings registered significant energy spikes on their EMF detectors, and the pair admitted that there was something about the two buildings that spoke to them—call it a ghost hunter's intuition.

Of course, they just made Dave more skeptical. First of all, how could there be EMF readings coming out of buildings that hadn't had any power running through them for years? And as for ghost hunter's intuition…c'mon.

With a bit more time to kill, the entourage continued over the compound. Jason and Grant were combing the place with their EMF detectors when they received unusually high readings, the highest yet. But when they told Dave and Matt about the EMF anomalies, the MTV guys responded with more skepticism. "Are you sure those things are totally accurate?" Dave asked. When Jason looked closely at the EMF meter and announced the data showed that there was some form of energy source right in the building, Dave was dubious and balked at it. "Yeah, guys, but what could possibly be causing that? Like I said before, none of these buildings have had power in them for—"

Before he'd been able to finish, an alarm bell suddenly went off right in the room they were standing in. Dave dropped his flashlight and practically jumped onto Jason's shoulders. Matt was similarly startled, though unlike his boss, he hadn't completely lost his composure. They all looked to the source of the racket: a single fire alarm clanging away on the wall in front of them.

"We've got to find the power source!" Jason called over the ringing.

The group found what they believed to be the basement door, and they waited for Dave to pick up his flashlight from where he'd dropped it before descending the stairs, hoping that they would find the building's fuse box. Their gut was right, and before long they stumbled upon the control panel. The alarm was still ringing when they reached the room, but the control box was a tangled mess of wires jutting from the panel like an explosion suspended indefinitely. Half the wires were too corroded to be of any use, and the other half were disconnected. Yet before they were able to take a closer look, the alarm stopped, just like that. Standing in front of the jumble of wires, Grant looked at Dave and Matt with a smile. "There ya go, guys," he said smiling. "Completely disconnected."

The decay and disarray of the wires was clear proof of what Dave had been saying all along: that there was no power in the building. "But I don't get it," he stammered. "How did the…?" He wasn't able to finish the question. Looking at Jason and Grant as though for the first time,

The paranormal team ran down to the basement to find the fuse box for the alarm.

the producer conceded that he was out of his depth. "Hey...you guys are the real deal, aren't you?"

Dave and Matt were eager to be out of the building as soon as possible after that, but they'd be back later on that night to shoot the segment. They were now in a well lit room by several filming lights, and there were production people running about, but something about the building still didn't feel right. Dave was telling Jason and Grant about how he was creeped out by the place, when his assistant came running up to the trio. Matt was breathless and looked as white as a…well…a ghost.

Concerned, Dave asked what was wrong. Matt was trembling and pointed toward the room he'd just come from. "In there," he stammered. "I was just in that room by myself, setting up equipment, when I saw something out of the corner of my eye!"

"Saw something?" the producer echoed. "What did you see?"

"I'm not sure what it was," the assistant replied, obviously still shaken. "It kind of looked like a person was standing there. I thought that maybe it was one of you guys who'd just walked in the room. But when I turned to look at who it was, it was gone…vanished!" Nevertheless, Matt swore that somebody had been there. He was sure of it.

If he was worried about coming across as crazy, Matt needn't have worried. Jason and Grant had heard these stories countless times before, and this sort of thing was exactly why they spent so much of their spare time investigating. "Let's go check it out," Jason said, and he and Grant walked into the dark hall that Matt had just come from. Dave and Matt followed close behind.

The first thing Jason noticed was the temperature. "It's definitely colder in here than it was in the hall," the experienced ghost hunter said to his colleague.

Grant looked down at his thermometer. "Yeah, I'm reading 42 degrees, about 20 degrees colder than in the other rooms."

Jason asked Matt where he'd seen the figure. "Over there," Matt responded, shakily pointing to the far corner. Jason cast his eyes around the room for a few moments before turning back to Dave and Matt. "Well, gentlemen, I'd suggest that you set up at least one video camera in this room here." He explained that the temperature drop was a common indicator of a supernatural presence drawing energy from its surroundings. Given the significant temperature drop, Jason reasoned that there was definitely a strong presence in the room.

A presence was likely still there, Grant was quick to add, which was enough for Matt, who briskly rubbed his arms and announced that the room was a bit too chilly for his comfort. Realizing that his assistant was more frazzled than he was letting on, Dave ordered a coffee break to allow his crew to fortify themselves. He was a skeptic before he arrived, and he hadn't expected the hospital to have such an effect on him, or his crew.

In the end, everyone had to agree that the FEAR pilot was a success, featuring genuinely creepy sequences and spawning a series that would continue for two full seasons. Everyone involved in its creation benefited from the experience. While Dave and his crew were able to capture memorable footage under Jason and Grant's direction, the two ghost hunters experienced what it was like to investigate a site under the glare of television cameras. The fact that they're currently hosting the nationally run *Ghost Hunters* says a lot about how successful they've become. As for the ghosts in the Fairfield Hills hospital, there was little Jason, Grant, Dave or the television cameras could do for them. And for all we know, they're still there, haunting the dismal grounds of the former hospital, without any ghost hunters, television producers or cameramen to appreciate their efforts.

Ghost Hunters' Glossary

ANGELS: Derived from the Greek word *angelos* ("messenger"), angels are the celestial messengers and guardians of a deity; though commonly associated with Christianity, angels are common to many religions. They are immaterial beings, sexless creatures of pure consciousness that possessed a knowledge no mortal could ever even hope to comprehend.

CLAIRAUDIENT: An individual with the ability to perceive sound or words beyond the range of hearing. These sounds can come from outside sources such as spirits or other entities. Clairaudience is said to be a form of channeling messages through audible thought patterns.

COLD SPOTS: Commonly associated with haunted sites, a cold spot is said to result from a ghost absorbing the necessary energy to materialize from its surroundings. They are usually quite localized and are 10 or more degrees cooler than the surrounding area.

DEMON: In Christian theology, demons are the instruments of evil, the fallen angels cast out of heaven with Lucifer. They exist for no other purpose but to torment and torture the living through abuse, assault and possession. However, in other cultures, demons are not nearly so malicious. To the Greeks, *daimons* (translated, the word means "divine power") served as intermediaries between mortals and the gods of Mount Olympus.

ECTOPLASM: A term popularized in the film *Ghostbusters*, ectoplasm is said to be a white, sticky goo-like substance with a smell resembling ozone. It is, hypothetically, a dense bio-energy used by spirits to materialize as ghosts. Its existence has never been proven.

EMF: An electromagnetic field, or EMF, is associated with an electric charge in motion. Many paranormal researchers equate an EMF with paranormal activity, believing that ghosts generate high levels of electromagnetic energy through their activities.

ESP: Extrasensory Perception, or ESP, describes the ability to perceive and receive information without the use of any of the usual five senses: sight, touch, smell, hearing and taste. Not surprisingly, ESP is often referred to as the sixth sense.

EVP: Electronic Voice Phenomena, or EVP, is a process through which the voices of the dead are captured on an audiocassette. How the process works is a bit of a mystery, but it usually involves placing a tape recorder at a haunted site. When played back, the voices of the dead should be clear on the recording and should not be confused with background noise or static.

EXORCISM: An exorcism is the purging of a person, place or thing that has been possessed by a demon or other unnatural force. It is normally carried out under the close supervision of a religious official, thoroughly trained and capable.

GEIGER COUNTER: An instrument that detects and measures radioactivity, or the spontaneous emission of energy from certain elements. This device searches for fluctuations in Alpha, Beta, Gamma and X-ray radiation, which point to a disturbance in spirit energy.

GHOST: Derived from the German word *geist* and the Dutch word *geest*, a ghost is the physical manifestation of an individual's disembodied spirit. It may appear as a figure, but a ghost can also manifest itself through smells, sounds and other sensations. At the heart of any belief concerning ghosts is the idea of a separation between the physical body and the metaphysical soul. The body perishes, though the soul does not.

MATERIALIZATION: The process through which seemingly solid objects or individuals appear out of thin air. It was a popular and well-documented phenomenon during the earliest years of Spiritualism, when mediums commonly caused objects like coins and cups to materialize.

ORBS: Though they may vary in shape, color and size, orbs are most commonly round in shape and whitish gray in color and are usually, though not always, found in photographs taken during a haunting or at a haunted site. They are believed to represent the spirit of the dead. Because dust, moisture and lens flare can easily be confused with orbs, some critics have argued that orbs may not be enough proof to legitimize a haunting.

OUIJA BOARD: An instrument that allegedly can be used to contact or channel spirits of the deceased. It is usually a wooden or cardboard device inscribed with the alphabet, the words "yes" and "no" and the numbers 0 to 9. There is usually a slideable apparatus on rotating castors or wheels with a pointer. The operators of the board place their fingers lightly on the slideable device and wait for it to move.

PARANORMAL: Any event that cannot be explained or defined through accepted scientific knowledge is said to be beyond what is normal. It is, therefore, paranormal.

POLTERGEIST: A combination of two German words, *poltern* (to knock) and *geist* (spirit), a poltergeist is characterized by its bizarre and mischievous behavior. Activities of a poltergeist include, but are not limited to, the moving of furniture, the throwing of objects and the rapping and knocking of walls. A poltergeist may also be responsible for terrible odors and cries. Typically, the activities of a poltergeist appear unfocused, pointless and completely random.

POSSESSION: A condition in which all of an individual's faculties fall under the control of an external force, such as a demon or deity. An individual possessed by a demon may alter his or her voice, even his or her appearance, and be fearful of religious symbols.

REVENANT: From the French *revenir* (to return), a revenant is a ghost that appears shortly after its physical death. Usually, it will only appear a few times, perhaps even just once, before disappearing from the earth forever.

SPIRITUALISM: A movement that originated in the United States in 1848, Spiritualism is a religion whose beliefs are centered upon the idea that communication with the dead is altogether possible. By the late 19th century, spiritualism had become popular throughout the United States. Its popularity ebbed in the early 20th century as many of the religion's earliest mediums were exposed as frauds, but rose again after World War I. It is still popular today.

THERMOGRAPH: A self-recording thermometer that traces temperature variations over time.

TRANCE: A trance is essentially an altered state of consciousness in which the individual, though not asleep, is barely aware of his or her immediate environment. There is some speculation that during a trance, the body enters a state that hovers somewhere between life and death, which frees the mind to explore a higher realm and gain spiritual insight.